Editor-in-Chief and Founder:
Lyndon H. LaRouche, Jr.
Editorial Board: *Lyndon H. LaRouche, Jr. , Helga
Zepp-LaRouche, Robert Ingraham, Tony
Papert, Gerald Rose, Dennis Small, Jeffrey
Steinberg, William Wertz*
Co-Editors: *Robert Ingraham, Tony Papert*
Managing Editor: *Nancy Spannaus*
Technology: *Marsha Freeman*
Books: *Katherine Notley*
Ebooks: *Richard Burden*
Graphics: *Alan Yue*
Photos: *Stuart Lewis*
Circulation Manager: *Stanley Ezrol*

INTELLIGENCE DIRECTORS
Counterintelligence: *Jeffrey Steinberg, Michele
Steinberg*
Economics: *John Hoefle, Marcia Merry Baker,
Paul Gallagher*
History: *Anton Chaitkin*
Ibero-America: *Dennis Small*
Russia and Eastern Europe: *Rachel Douglas*
United States: *Debra Freeman*

INTERNATIONAL BUREAUS
Bogotá: *Miriam Redondo*
Berlin: *Rainer Apel*
Copenhagen: *Tom Gillesberg*
Houston: *Harley Schlanger*
Lima: *Sara Madueño*
Melbourne: *Robert Barwick*
Mexico City: *Gerardo Castilleja Chávez*
New Delhi: *Ramtanu Maitra*
Paris: *Christine Bierre*
Stockholm: *Ulf Sandmark*
United Nations, N.Y.C.: *Leni Rubinstein*
Washington, D.C.: *William Jones*
Wiesbaden: *Göran Haglund*

ON THE WEB
e-mail: eirns@larouchepub.com
www.larouchepub.com
www.executiveintelligencereview.com
www.larouchepub.com/eiw
Webmaster: *John Sigerson*
Assistant Webmaster: *George Hollis*
Editor, Arabic-language edition: *Hussein Askary*

EIR (ISSN 0273-6314) *is published weekly
(50 issues), by EIR News Service, Inc.,
P.O. Box 17390, Washington, D.C. 20041-0390.
(703) 777-9451*

European Headquarters: E.I.R. GmbH, Postfach
Bahnstrasse 9a, D-65205, Wiesbaden, Germany
Tel: 49-611-73650
Homepage: http://www.eirna.com
e-mail: eirna@eirna.com
Director: Georg Neudecker

Montreal, Canada: 514-461-1557

Denmark: EIR - Danmark, Sankt Knuds Vej 11,
basement left, DK-1903 Frederiksberg, Denmark.
Tel.: +45 35 43 60 40, Fax: +45 35 43 87 57. e-mail:
eirdk@hotmail.com.

Mexico City: EIR, Sor Juana Inés de la Cruz 242-2
Col. Agricultura C.P. 11360
Delegación M. Hidalgo, México D.F.
Tel. (5525) 5318-2301
eirmexico@gmail.com

Canada Post Publication Sales Agreement
#40683579

Postmaster: Send all address changes to *EIR*, P.O.
Box 17390, Washington, D.C. 20041-0390.

Signed articles in *EIR* represent the views of the
authors, and not necessarily those of the Editorial
Board.

British Genocide And War

The Immediate, Grave Danger Of Genocide

Jan. 14—The United States and the world are facing an immediate grave danger. President Obama's State of the Union address demonstrated that he is completely out of control, Lyndon LaRouche said today. The speech was a total fraud, and anyone accepting Obama's lies is opening the United States up for total destruction. On behalf of the British, Obama is ready to blow up the United States altogether. This is an immediate option. The issue of Wall Street's crimes is actually a cover for the fact that the United States as a whole is being set up for genocide. This is the British policy of genocide, and the current Pope has been thoroughly suckered into it.

It is not just Obama who is doing the killing; Obama is only the lead dog. It's the British,—the British Empire.

The Dance of Death by Michael Wolgemut, 1493.

And of course people are frightened; maybe they're not frightened enough. But in any case, we have to tell the truth.

The planned genocide is the secret of the massive COP21 "climate-change" conference in Paris last November-December, with its estimated 50,000 participants representing 196 nations. But no binding treaty could possibly be reached,—What was its purpose then? It was the mass-declaration of intention for this genocide. It was to rally the troops for the scheduled "big kill." It was the Dance of Death.

And this Pope's May 2015 encyclical, *Laudato Si'*, calling for humankind to be sacrificed for the sake of the "climate," was exactly the same thing. The Pope has come under British direction and control; he is being used by a British operation. He's committing crimes.

The thrust of the genocide is aimed squarely at the trans-Atlantic region. But it is accompanied by the British threat to destroy Asia by war. That is what Obama is working on in the western Pacific; the Russians understand this completely.

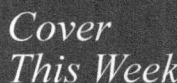

EIR Contents

www.larouchepub.com Volume 43, Number 4, January 22, 2016

Cover This Week

The mentality behind the British Army's practice of blowing up Indian mutineers—by tying them to the muzzles of cannon—is the same that underlies the Empire's drive for war and genocide today.

I. Time To Face the Facts

Overcome Your Fears; Our Enemy Is the British Empire—Period!

by Lyndon LaRouche

Over a three-day period, from Jan. 14 to Jan. 16, Lyndon LaRouche engaged in a series of public and private discussions during which he directly addressed the actual nature of the current strategic crisis, as well as the fear which is preventing both elected officials and the citizenry from acting in a bold and appropriate fashion. We begin with quotations from Mr. LaRouche to a private assembly on Jan. 16:

Jan. 16 Private Meeting

LaRouche: People are trying to pick details. And trying to pick details does not show you what the real picture is. And that's the point. But what's happened is that the world at large is being fooled by details of this nature. What the reality is,—the whole thing is created on the basis of the continuity of the British Empire. So, the British Empire is the target you've got to pay attention to. You've got to understand the British Empire, and everything that's happening is that.

Look at what's happening with this crazy pope! He's a nut! He's insane; he's a killer, and his vows are those of a killer. And he's a leading pope, nominally. Who runs it? The British Empire runs it! And all of this stuff is based on the problems defined by the British Empire. The whole thing is a British Empire scheme. It doesn't mean it's a "plan" that they have, as such, that's going to win. But, they've decided to play that game.

THE BRITISH EMPIRE

THE BRITISH COMMONWEALTH

CURRENT WAR FLASHPOINTS

NATO

DOMINATED BY LONDON'S DOPE INC. NARCO-TERRORISM APPARATUS OR THE SPECULATIVE BANKING SYSTEM

LPAC

British imperial domination over the planet as of January 2015.

And everything is being done within the context of that game.

And I think our organization gets fooled into believing that these things are the keystones; they are not. What do you have to do? If you remove the British royal family, the problem's over. Therefore don't try to say, "this detail, this detail, this thing is the issue"; it is not! There's only one issue: Eliminate the British Empire! Eliminate everything it stands for; shut it down.

Don't worry about the details. The detail is: Are we going to end the existence of the British Empire, or not? That's it! There is no other issue. All the other issues, are only superficial, in terms of their characterization. If you look at the history of mankind—Bertrand Russell! Bertrand Russell, remember him? This is how it was run. What happened? At the beginning of the Twentieth Century, Bertrand Russell came in, and everything that was happening was defined by Bertrand Russell! You had almost no one who was not a stooge for Bertrand Russell. We had a few people who were against him, but they were eliminated soon enough.

Only One Issue

You've got to understand there is not "this thing, and this thing, and then this thing, and then this thing." No! It's nonsense! Reality is: the British Empire has set the whole thing up. What do you think has happened in the United States? What do you think has happened with the people of the United States? It's that It's the British Empire. But people in our organization are trying to adapt to this scenario, these kinds of scenarios, and they're idiots. Most of our members, on this question, behave like idiots.

There's one issue: the British Empire, period. That's the only subject. What do we do about the British Empire? Everything else is just talk, just talk, a distraction. When people come in here, come to me and say, "Well, here's the latest information," I begin to groan. Because, when people come in with something "new"— "Oh, this is the big new issue"—bunk! It's not the "new big issue.'

Look at the course of history. Don't look at what you say "so-and-so does this, so-and-so says that, so-and-so talks about that, so-and-so believes that"—it's all nonsense! We really should know what the story is, but we talk ourselves into these "this, that, and this thing, and that thing, and this thing"—it's nonsense, it has no reality to it. The point is to get rid of that kind of "rut stuff" out of your mind!

The British Empire dominates the planet! It's still doing it! How do you think the Green policy is going through, and how far is the Green policy operating? How far is it operating, right now? Now, what's the Green policy? It is entirely the British System! It is nothing but the British System. So, don't go looking for explanations, *per se*. You have to sink the British Empire! The other stuff is simply a way of chattering, and the result is simply fantasies. Most of our people get stuck into pure fantasies, not reality. .. What's the reality? What is the real thing that's going on? All around the world—the British Empire…

The people who are brainwashed in the British System don't like to say so; they don't like to admit it, but it's true. If you think carefully about people in the United States, they're brainwashed. The typical American is a brainwashed victim of the British system. Think carefully. Think about Wall Street. What's Wall Street? It dominates the country, the nation. Well, who does that? Ha, ha! Wall Street, what's Wall Street? Wall Street is an expression of the British Empire. The culture, think about the culture, the kind of culture—the changes in culture—that have gone on inside the United States itself.

Members of the United States are a pack of idiots. Why are they a pack of idiots? Because they want to follow these ideas: "Oh, this is the thing that's important!" Why is it important? Well, because they're being told that it's important. All these subjects, these fads, even the design of your costumes you wear, that's all they are. It's fake. It's a game. The best thing to do, if we get desperate, we take all the British agents in one swoop. And then we will have a better kind of world.

But don't get into this thing about "this guy, and this guy, and this guy has this, and this guy has this"—it's chatter. There are a lot of facts that we can pick out, and we sometimes do pick out, but when you're defining policy and strategy, that's where most of our members, and most of the people of the world, get fooled. They're suckers. They want to "explain," they want to come up with a "story": "Oh, we have the latest story; we have the latest evidence; we have the latest this; we got this information; we're watching this guy very carefully." Boom! Nothing! It doesn't mean a damn thing! It's a stunt.

I've seen this thing, and watched it—the typical

American is an idiot. And that's the good side!

Why Most People Are Idiots

Most of the Presidents of the United States were trash and worse. It's a fact; so why are you listening, saying we've got to check on these guys? Why not just say, "Yes, we know about them. They're trash?" That's the end of the conversation. If it's popular, it stinks. If it's popular, it's rotten. Rotten things are just like that. The education system—the people are rotten, that we get in the universities. What is going on in the West Coast in general, what's the culture? What do they produce? It's awful!

And therefore, the idea that you can somehow adapt to these kinds of recipes, these kind of perspectives . . . take culture, music. What culture? What culture? Dead. Rotten. Practical people are inherently stupid, so why are you listening to them? They're inherently stupid. I've known that for a very long time, but some of you guys didn't catch on to that. "I learned in school." What do you get in schools? Crap! How do you get a degree in university? Crap!

Look at the record, and then think of the change that occurred at the beginning of the Twentieth Century, which is dominated by Bertrand Russell. That's your culture, and you believe in it. Why do you believe in it? Because you want to be popular. What do you get by being popular? Well, various kinds of diseases. That's what popularity is for, to be a vehicle of diseases.

We have to stand apart from that. We cannot say that we have gimmicks. "This is something that will work for us, this is something that will be useful to us." Forget it! Popular opinion. And the problem with the American people is they talk too much. Why are they talking too much? Because they're idiots! Why are they idiots? Because they believe in discussing things, and they all assemble to discuss things. And what are they discussing? Idiocy!

You have to learn that. Anyone who went to schools and universities and so forth, should have been warned that this thing is a fake. But they would say, "Yes, you have to take this into account, you've got to take this into account." Sometimes, you have to terrify these bastards. They're so stupid the only way you can get

National Foundations to End Senior Hunger

Genocide in America: A scene in McDowell County, West Virginia, scene of shut down mines, shut down schools, and the highest rate of heroin addiction in the country.

them to think is to terrify them. Otherwise, their brains don't work. . . .

If you want to deal with the enemy, you've got to frighten the enemy with the effect of what the enemy intends to do. I've had a little fun with that. Most people are idiots. Why are they idiots? Because they want to be practical. The only way you can become an idiot is to be practical.

But this whole thing about being practical, it disgusts me inherently. I want to hit something when I hear about something practical. It's corruption, actually. It's absolutely corruption. It's trying to adapt to something as showmanship; and it's always a fraud. And you can't blame the dogs for that. Sometimes, I think they should pee on something, because it's better than the alternative.

We have to get rid of this shibboleth kind of stuff.

Jan. 14 Fireside Chat

The following remarks were delivered by Lyndon LaRouche during his Thursday, <u>Jan. 14 Fireside Chat</u>, the first response is to an individual who described the current hellish conditions in the State of West Virginia, and the second is a response to an individual who questioned both what is holding back the effort to remove Barack Obama from office, and what can be done about the corruption of elected officials:

LaRouche: OK, good. Let's look at this thing in a practical way, because you've gone through a number of facts which are all true. *But!* we don't have to have any of those problems! We don't! if we change the Presidency now, and if we go back in the direction of what we have known how to do during the course of my lifetime. I was born in 1922, and I have a pretty good knowledge of what the history is. I wasn't there in 1922, because I had just been born then, but I have pretty good knowledge about what this is all about.

Now, this is what happened. We start with Bertrand Russell, whose career began at the beginning of the Twentieth Century. And he was the most evil man that was ever born, up to this point at this time.

So the problem is, we are still—in the United States and beyond the United States, in general, the population of the United States, of South America, of Central America, of Europe today, Europe as such,—Putin is in better shape than the rest of Europe is, for example. China is in excellent condition, compared to what the United States is today.

Now if we were to say, we're going to throw out what Bertrand Russell represents—and that was *really evil* stuff—and if we say we're going to change that, now we've got a problem. You've got students, young students, middle school age students, all kinds of students; well, most of these students are pretty stupid. That is, most of the students today, in the United States in particular, who are being educated, or getting promotions and so forth on the basis of being educated, they're pretty stupid. They're almost hopelessly stupid.

Especially in California. California's the area—they have a Governor over there in California, and he really is a mess, and he's destroying California. We have to get rid of him! Because California is capable of reversing its direction. We have a number of people who I was closely associated with in California. They are very effective people, but unfortunately, we have a Governor in California at this time, who is really a Satanic force. If you remove him from his position as a Satanic force, things get better. If you go in cooperation with other nations which are trying to do the same thing as China, for example, you'll find that there'll be a sudden reversal of the kind of degeneracy which has hit the United States in particular over the entire period since the beginning of the Twentieth Century.

That will be changed. Remember what happened: Remember the space program, before Obama killed it, all these things; all these good things that we used to do can be brought back. But we have to have the determination to make sure they *do* come back. Because we cannot tolerate what is happening to the miners in West Virginia and so forth. You can't accept that. We have to change it.

So, why don't we just change it? How do we do that? Well, I'm willing to do my stint for that operation. Get *rid* of the bums. Get rid of the idiocy, get rid of the degeneracy which hits most of the members of our population. The biggest problem in the United States is the galloping degeneration of the living members of this nation. We have to change that. We *can* change it. We have to resolve to change it. And that's the mission that we've just got to take on.

You will find that China will cooperate with us in this. Russia will cooperate. Certain other nations of the planet will cooperate. But the main thing we have to get rid of are two things: First, get rid of the British system, just eliminate it, *absolutely!* And then eliminate what's rotten inside the United States.

And you will find that happened with Franklin Roosevelt in his administration. What he did is, he made works of genius in his term of office as President. All the great things that were built in that period tell us, all we have to do is get rid of the bums and give a chance to the people who need help and will take it; and we will rebuild the economy of the United States.

LaRouche: I would say this, I would say, well, here's what the situation is: Wall Street is hopelessly bankrupt. Not only is Wall Street bankrupt, but the entire trans-Atlantic community is bankrupt, *hopelessly bankrupt.*

Now, that doesn't mean that the nation's territory has to also go down. It does not. All you have to do, is get rid of *all* the interests which are associated with Wall Street in the United States and throughout the world. Now, if you shut these guys down, fire them, tell them they have no rights, no privileges, they don't deserve to eat, things like that, because poor people have to have something to eat for a change. And if we go at this thing right, we will find that the confidence that we can bestir, by challenging the evil which is represented by Obama; for example, if you get rid of Obama, and if you tell people Obama has actually been removed—well, see most of the parents of those who have been *killed* by Obama! That is, what has happened. there's a mass of people who are regularly murdered by Obama personally, on Tuesdays.

What is holding everything back is, people are *scared*. They're scared because Obama is killing people! He's killing citizens of the United States. He terrifies people from the most powerful economic interests in the United States. They are terrified by Obama! Now, if you take Obama, and you put him in prison for the crimes he's committed—and he has to stay in prison—he's not going to have much influence on the life of humanity. So, the best thing to do, let's shuffle this guy into a deep prison, and give him a chance to think about his sins, his evils. And let the sins take over.

You'll find that once you close down Wall Street and close these racketeers and murders—and Obama is a murderer. He's a criminal, he's a murderer. Close him down, get rid of him. Let him go someplace else. He wants to travel, let him try Mars; it might be a good place for him. Of course, he won't last too long, and therefore the pollution won't persist too long.

But the point is that we have to do it. And we *can* do it, and we *must* do it. We can do it. Just stop being scared, or not that scared.

Jan. 16 New York City Meeting

Two days after the nationwide Fireside Chat, Lyndon LaRouche spoke on Jan. 16 before a Town Hall Meeting in New York City, where he further investigated the question of the fear and the cowardice that is holding back the citizenry. We present excerpts of this dialogue below:

LaRouche: It's a good time to have this kind of thing, right today. As you probably some of us here are watching you, and watching me and so forth. And we've augmented some of our attendance here, and why don't we just go ahead and do what we're supposed to, and see what happens?...

Question: One of the things that I was thinking, there are many events coming up where Congress people will be speaking, or holding things on their own, and if we get to more of their constituents,—I plan to talk to some of the people who are with me, some who are in this room, actually, and go to an event that's being held by Mr. Jeffries coming up soon.

So if we think in that way, to get to the constituents to make *them* force the Congress people to do the right thing also, and confront them on their territory and make the phones calls, do those kinds of things where people are actually helping us to make them do the right thing.

LaRouche: That's what we're trying to do. It's what we have to do. And it's a tough row to ride, because they are scared. They're intimidated, they're frightened, and they don't have much courage. If you get a little bit out of them, it may be useful. But you have to recognize the fact that we have a very cowardly organization to deal with. They're frightened.

But we have to understand that Obama is the problem, because Obama's role has been that of a killer. Look, here's a man, Obama, he kills people! He kills people; every Tuesday, he kills people. And that is not conducive to peaceful and productive discussion. And therefore, the problem is of that nature. And I think you have to take a little bit of his scalp—now, it doesn't mean you have to take his scalp, because I don't think you want greasy scalps. But in any case, that is where the problem lies.

In general, the citizens of the United States are very cowardly. They will not tell the truth; they will back off, they will duck, they will do all these kinds of tricks; and it's very difficult to get them to be honest. And they usually are not very honest. They'll say "Yes, but..." the old billy-goat song, "yes, but... yes, but... yes, but...."

So it's a difficult problem. But I think from an organization such as this one here, which is a little less than cowardly, we might get a little bit of more action here, from the people assembled here, than we did from the Congress by a long shot.

Question: Greetings, Lyndon. You mentioned the 28 pages previously, and the lack of courage in the Congress. And back during the Vietnam era, there was a Senator named Mike Gravel who brought the Pentagon Papers to the attention of a Congressional body. And although a lot of people wanted to punish him, they couldn't, because he had immunity when he presented it to a Congressional body.

Now today, most of our Congressmen haven't had the courage, yet, to even read the 28 pages. And those who have read them are more or less shocked. They can't speak about the content of what they read, they can't take notes, they can't bring in cell phones, or cameras. They have to read it in front of a guard.

My question to you: Do we, or can we identify a man, or woman, in the Congress, either in the House or the Senate, who has the courage to stand up on the floor of Congress, and to basically recite what they remem-

When Americans had courage: The signing of the Declaration of Independence, depicted here by artist John Trumbull, put the signers under potential sentence of death.

ber of the 28 pages; to let the entire world know, who was at least in part responsible for the financing of 9/11, the terror that we're still under, through ISIS—no doubt it's still connected—to draw that line, at least to put that idea in the American public?

So I ask you again: can you, or can this group, identify an historical character, who now can step forward at this great time of crisis, and speak the truth as to what they've read in those pages, and identify the terrorists responsible, at least in part, for the 9/11 atrocities? Thank you.

The Problem is Gutlessness

LaRouche: Okay. Well, I know about this; other people know about this condition, and what is required. *But* amazingly, leading members of the Congress, haven't got the guts to say so. It's all true. It's known. We have leading members of Congress, or those who have been leading members of Congress, they know this. I know this. Other people know this. And that's the truth.

What's the problem? The problem is the problem of

Obama right now. It was the Bush family, now it's Obama. And Obama uses threats of *killing*. Obama is a specialist in *killing* members of Congress and similar kinds of people. And they're scared. Because they think that being killed by him has a factor of futility. They're frightened.

And because of the press—the press is frightened. *They* are frightened. And that's the problem. It's not that simple. We have a population in the United States which is *scared as Hell*. And when it comes to this issue, only a few will speak. Only a few.

Question: My question, or my response, is that we only need actually one to speak, publicly. The international papers, I'm sure, the media would pick that up, and, the United States media would be forced to pick it up. The Internet media certainly would pick it up, at least to some extent.

So we only have to identify one brave person. I think that many people are frightened, but that's not anything new. That's been happening all through history. People eventually step up to bat. You've been doing it for many years, many years.

LaRouche: Yes, but they won't do it; *they are scared!* And their fear is not unjustified. What happens is, every Tuesday, citizens of the United States are killed by order of the President. *This* President. And, it's that kind of fear.

Now there are other conditions of cowardice in the population. In other words, we're speaking of Manhattan. And people who are living in southern Manhattan, know all about this, understand it, but there are very few who find the ability to come up and speak it. *That's* the problem.

Question: You know, I think of the Founding Fathers and the fifty-six people who signed the Declaration of Independence, and they knew when they signed that they were basically signing their death warrant if they didn't succeed in the Revolution. And, I would think that, karmically, we have a tie into 1776, and that we *must* be able to identify at least one patriot amongst the Congressmen, and have that patriot stand forward, and we give him that support he needs.

LaRouche: The problem is, we have the *gutlessness* of most citizens of the United States, when it comes to their standing there. And the problem is, it's not just simple gutlessness. *They can be killed by the President of the United States*, that is, Obama. Obama will kill people on a minute's notice. And people don't know how to get out of the threat of being killed for speaking out.

Then you get a problem in the population more generally. They become collectively terrified. And it's very difficult to get members of Congress, or even ordinary citizens to tell the truth about tough matters. The United States is full of cowards. But they're not cowards, *per se;* they know that *Obama can kill them.* The smartest ones know that he can kill them. Obama can do it, and *has* done it, repeatedly. Every Tuesday, citizens of the United States are being *killed* by the order of Obama. On Tuesday.

So, it's going to take something a little tougher than we have, as an organizing process, to get this problem across. People know it! A good number of people *know* it. Very few people will speak it. Why? Because they think it's futile. Because they think that even their sacrifice of their own life will not work. And, that's the problem. So, the point is, *you've got to throw Obama out of office.* Throw him out of office!

Look what he's doing now. He's killing a whole bunch of citizens in various parts of the world, just killing them. And he's doing it; he's getting by with it. Germany won't fight. Other nations won't fight. Do you expect a citizen, who is not a potent citizen, to fight like that? They will talk about it in a certain way. They won't speak out for it.

We have turned our nation into a batch of cowards. But the cowardice is not unwarranted. And it's going to take some tough work to solve that problem. It has to be solved, but it's not something that you can just do. You've got to make it happen, but you can't just make it happen arbitrarily. You really have to pull it off. And, if you can build that up mentally, that is a step in the right direction. But it's not something you can just pull off on the street. Unfortunately, that's true.

Cowards and Liars in Congress

Question: What do you think would be an appropriate approach toward Martin Luther King's birthday?

LaRouche: I think we have a chance of doing something about it. The opening is there. The question is how to get the mechanism to function because the thing is knowable. But what I'm impressed by is the fear of citizens.

Now, if you want to understand how serious that is, you have to take the name of Obama. Obama is actually the person who is chiefly responsible for the terror against the citizens of the United States themselves. Why? Because he *kills.* He kills on Tuesdays; he kills innocent citizens on Tuesdays. That's been his profession. And nobody steps in there and says, "you're not going to be killed." What they get is that the order is given, to kill them! Obama does it on Tuesdays!

And therefore you have to get a force of influence which can muster people to stand up with courage enough to deal with this problem. That's the problem. We have a nation of cowards, and that's the problem....

Question: Hi Lyn. I want to give a very brief report on what we did last week in Albany, where we're now moving, and we will have the Glass-Steagall resolution re-introduced in Albany. And this will be the third year we've had the Glass-Steagall resolution introduced, and what happens is that we have a good number of people who are co-sponsors, but the resolution is never taken out of committee.

Now, in terms of what you're talking about, about how to get people to deal with the fear, I think this is the critical question, and I want to tell you a short story.

We met with a State Senator during the Summer, who is from Harlem. And he wanted to introduce Glass-Steagall. He was going to put it in the Senate; he was going to write a letter, an op-ed in the *Amsterdam News*, and everything was moving, and he was going to read about Ferdinand Pecora, and get some guts on this thing. So then we didn't hear anything.

So we went on Tuesday to his office and talked to his aide. His aide had told us during the Summer, well, there's not enough people backing it, okay. It's good, we're for it. Well, this time we walked in and the aide was very happy. The Senator had endorsed Bernie Sanders, and Sanders was just in New York talking about Glass-Steagall. And so he was ready to re-write the resolution, and he was ready to move. And then the Senator came in.

Now just to put it in context: On the wall of the Senator's office, there's a poster. And on one side is Martin Luther King, and it says "The Dreamer," and on the other side is Barack Obama, and it says, "The Dream." [audience gasps]

And what happened in our discussion is, at first the Senator was talking about introducing Glass-Steagall, and how it would work, and how do you explain it. And then he became more and more and more enraged, and he was attacking the way we were talking about it, and he said, "People in my district can't understand this. They can't understand it; this is arrogant to talk about derivatives. People don't know what derivatives are. You can't talk about derivatives."

And on the housing crisis—which in Harlem is off the charts, where people are being shoved out by gentrification—he said "I don't see any connection between Glass-Steagall and housing," and he said, "Look we've met for an hour, I've given you all this time." And we fought it out.

But nonetheless, what we didn't say, and I think it's

MLive.com

Genocide in America: The poisonous water in Flint, Michigan—the result of Wall Street budget-cutting—brought these citizens into the streets on Jan. 18.

very important to what you are saying today; we didn't say to him, *"You are terrified!* of what you've got up on your wall. That's the problem!"

And instead we tended to argue it out, but I think the point you're making, if people really think about it, and I'm thinking about it because I know we have to do this differently; we have to say what you're saying, and which is actually true, that there is enormous fear. And there's fear about Obama, there's fear that you're dealing with a killer, and there's fear about the fact that you put him in office, and that you continue to try to support him. And I think perhaps if we're going to move this thing in Albany, to actually get Glass-Steagall voted on, we have to bring this question up. And I wanted to both tell you that, and see if you have any comments.

LaRouche: I do have a comment. The point is that, yes, these conditions exist. No doubt about it. It happens.

Members of Congress are not only cowardly, they are liars. Look, if somebody comes into the office there of a member of Congress, or in another state, if they come there and they raise this question, the truth is, *that question presents the truth.* Everybody knows it. That is, if they wish to know it. And therefore, the people who say that are lying. The members of Congress and State Representatives who are taking that position are lying. They *know* they're lying, fully. And they continue to lie. Because they say their interest requires them to lie. And the only way you can do it is, you've got to find the circumstance, under which you can just say that outright. "Well, we know you're lying. We know you're lying. But we'd just like to have you tell the truth a couple of times."

And that's the only way you can deal with it. Then they will get very upset, they'll denounce you in all kinds of directions, and say this was insane, this was terrible, this was not decent, "I'm a respectable member of Congress, I have these rights, you can't say these things about *me!*"

You say, "well, *aren't* you lying?" [laughter] And they just walk out of the room and tear things up. They're terrified.

The Citizens Have Lost Their Guts

Question: We've got a big week coming up in New York. And my question to you in terms of the drive—the removal of Obama—we've got the two main issues: Wall Street being crushed by Glass-Steagall, and taking the 28 pages to a much-needed higher level. How do you propose, how do you suggest, we move, now, and in the next few weeks?

LaRouche: You are faced with a threat which is a most credible threat, to destroy everything that you have! And it's there right now! What Obama is doing, what the Wall Street crowd is doing, is they're destroying the very life existence of the citizens of the United States, who are faced with actions which will kill them.

Now, right now, for example there are whole categories of people who are employed citizens of economic function. And they kill each other! They literally kill each other, or they kill themselves; because they're terrified. And on that basis, very few people among them have the courage to live! People tend to die because they are afraid and they want to get rid of being afraid *by dying.* And that's what's come to the people of the United States.

And they can't trust the Congress, they can't trust the members of Congress, they can't trust the society, and they're being killed! And the rate of killing of citizens is rising. And it seems that virtually nothing is being done about that.

Now, we're on the edge of the worst and most dangerous war that has ever been fought by mankind. We're on the edge of Russia and China against the British Empire, what the British Empire represents, or what Obama represents as well. Those are the problems. And if the citizens have the guts, they'll respond to that.

But the citizens have lost their guts. They've been taken away from them. The members of their families are terrified. They become cowards regularly. Now me, old man me, well I say these things. I have been in the practice of saying these kinds of things. But very few people—I'm not saying that I'm the greatest hero—that's not the case. *I understand, more deeply than most citizens of the United States do.* And the only problem is the cowardice is of a very specific kind: "Look, it's not that bad."

"You're saying it's bad, it's not that bad. *It's not that bad!"* [pounds the table, laughter]

And that's what the problem is. Cowardice! And we have to help people get back their courage.

Question: Mr. LaRouche, I had a discussion with a few friends of mine and I brought up the Hill-Burton system. And with the Glass-Steagall, how would rebuilding the Hill-Burton system work?

LaRouche: I can identify that very quickly. I'm very familiar with that. Look, the problem here is cowardice which is induced in the citizens. They don't want to take on those issues. They don't want to take on, also, the issues which *involve themselves.* They don't want to take on the recognition of their *own cowardice.* Therefore, they don't want to admit that they're cowards.

Look, you have people who are dying. They are killing themselves. In labor union activities they're there, they know this. They're being killed. They're dying. The rate of death of people in these qualities of production, of manufacturing, and things like that—they're dying, they're collapsing. They *wish* to die. They do things that show that they wish to die, because they want to get this over with.

Iif you can induce people to become cowards, then you can make them to do whatever you want them do. And that's what the problem is.

'Practical Measures' Don't Work

Many of these people who were working people, who had professions as working people, they quit. They were cowards. And they actually acted in order to induce their own *death!* In order to end the noise of dying. And that's what's happening. And if you can't solve that problem and end that problem, mankind becomes a collection of cowards, the worst kind of cowards. They won't face the truth.

They take drugs. They take drugs in order to kill themselves. People who are working people kill them-

Genocide in America: Drug-related death rates among "non-Hispanic" whites within the 25-34 age group, both men and women, have increased 500% since 1999, according to a recent New York Times *analysis of Centers for Disease Control data.*

selves to get rid of life because of their cowardice. And this is the thing we face, and therefore the question is *how do we change that kind of reaction*? The number of people who are working people, who are trade unionists, for example, and similar categories—the death rate among them is increasing at an accelerating rate. And to a large degree it is voluntary. They are *trying to escape from life*, from a life which is no longer enjoyable.

And therefore we have to go to a higher level of action, not practical measures. Practical measures never worked. Practical measures under these kinds of conditions were always a failure! They were always a bluff. They never meant anything. And when you have people and members of families who commit suicide in one form or the other, that's the most extreme kind of cowardice. Working people for whom the conditions of life are worsening, lose their guts. And my problem is, how do I do things which will *help them get back their guts?* Then they will do the best.

Question: I want to talk about this question of cowardice because it seems to me that since the death of FDR the American people have been *terrorized* under McCarthy, Truman's bombing of Japan, the death of Kennedy, the assassination of Malcolm X, the assassination of King, the assassination Bobby Kennedy. And this being the celebration of Martin Luther King's birthday, I think that it would be good if we use that,—when we're talking to these Congressmen,—that they have to

come up to that level, they have to come up and do the right thing.

The other thing I wanted to mention about FDR, is that in 1940 and 1944 when he gave his inaugural address, both times he referred to the fact that people make mistakes. And he said that he himself, as President had made mistakes. But he said, the scales of justice for mistakes are different, because if you have a good heart, a warm heart, that the scale of justice is on your side. But if you have a cold heart, that's bad.

Anyways, I just wanted to bring that up, and see what you thought about the idea of making from now to President's Day or earlier, the focus of getting these Congressmen to move?

LaRouche: Well, the problem was the FBI. The FBI was the thing that destroyed the United States. That's exactly what happened. And Obama is carrion left over from that stuff.

No, this has been the case. And the members of Congress have become increasingly cowardly, succession after succession. The willful degeneration of the members of Congress is among the most appalling experiences that I've ever witnessed.

Now, how did that happen? As the soldiers returned at the end of World War II, at the time of the so-called preliminary peace agreement, that's when the cowardice took over.

When I got back from doing service in Asia, I was promoted rapidly to a very lucrative position as a leader in economics in Manhattan. And then the FBI got rid of me. And what happened? A lot of people got the same treatment. And that's how it happened.

You had people who were privileged, ostensibly, and you had people who were treated as lower-level people. One group would do almost anything to get something, to get rewards whether they deserved them or not, and there was another group of people who were always the underdogs. And that's how the system worked.

The U.S.A. Has No Sovereignty

And that had happened already when I got back, out of military service. It already had happened! And the people I knew, in general, were sort of slaves. They were given the worst jobs, the worst employment opportunities, so forth, that's what was happening! That was being done by the citizens of the United States *against* the citizens of the United States! Under the leadership of Wall Street! Under the leadership of what? Of the FBI.

The greatest agency of hate, against the people of the United States, was the FBI! The FBI was the most murderously inclined element of the U.S. government.

Now, we're still fighting this! What do you think it is? What are the leading members of the Congress? They're the enemies of the people! By their voting! Take the vote that just passed, at the end of last year, it was an act of *treason* against the American people! Who did it?

The Congress!

So, these are the things that have to be said, openly and directly. And it's because people are afraid to talk about those things *in those terms*, that the very spoken words betray them.

Question: Good afternoon, Mr. LaRouche. I'm from the state of Connecticut. Meanwhile, on the battlefront last night, I went to see a movie, *The Big Short*. Just before it ended, I walked out and stood by the exit, and I had over 100 leaflets of our Glass-Steagall and Recovery, one of the older ones, and it was an opportunity of a lifetime, and it came to me in a dream. [applause]

My second thing—This is what I'm trying to do to help this fight: The economy of Connecticut has been destroyed by Wall Street, taxes without representation. I have set up meetings with the state representatives.... I will have meetings with them so we can push in what the constituents need, the Glass-Steagall. And they can write or call their elected officials. And this is my part. What is your ...

LaRouche: OK, I will respond to that. The problem here is, that we are governed by the British Empire. The United States *has no sovereignty!* No efficient sovereignty. You have some things that are called "sovereignty" in the United States, but *they ain't real*. And that has been the case ever since Franklin Roosevelt was being dumped before his death. In other words, once the election had occurred, the Republican Party had won; at that point, the United States' honor had collapsed, and has been collapsed ever since.

So therefore, the problem is not how do we explain how it should have worked or what the principle is. There *is* no principle! *There is no principle!*

The United States has always been, since that time, suffering the *wrongs* of life. That's been the course of life. Who ran it? The British Empire ran it! They ran it!

And people of the United States did duty for the British. That's how it worked. That's always been the case since that time.

Therefore, if you want to be honest, and also a little bit courageous, all you have to do, is say, "we're going to shut this thing down." For example, I make jokes about it, but it's true, it's a truthful joke, about Manhattan. Much of the stuff, the wealth of Manhattan is junk, it's trash! It's not worth anything to the human beings, to the people. People may like expensive buildings, they may like these kinds of things,—as long as they possess them! But they don't do anything for the human beings in general.

The education system, throughout the United States, is degenerating, and it's degenerating at an *accelerating rate*. The members of the Congress are degenerating at an accelerating rate.

China and Russia

So what is needed is an action on behalf of the United States and its people to bring an end to this crap! We are slaves of the British Empire, because the whole system is run from and by the *British Empire*. They run it! The Queen is still doing it. And the Queen has to be put in prison because she's stupid and therefore we can't have her running around in a condition like that, being a stupid person. This is not right.

So anyway, what runs our world? Does the United States run the world? No! *The British Empire controls the world!* It need not do so, however. If we in the United States say we're not going to have that any more, we just simply cancel it and the Queen goes out! But the people don't have the guts to do it—"Oh! The Queen! Oh!! The Queen!" Somebody comes up, and they faint, "Oh, the Queen is here, again!"

We fail to recognize the truth. And I've had some experience with the truth. As I said, I served in India, around India, as a GI. I got into trouble with the British, for which I'm very proud. I pulled something off and did some other things which got some people very excited, because I had the opportunity to say "this will work" and I would talk to the military people. We would discuss things. They said, "it's a good idea" until they found out I was doing it, and then they tried to pull me off it!

So I had a good life and a good perspective, and I was not a slave. But I turned around, went back to the United States and I found that I was suddenly a slave. An ordinary citizen, better known as a *slave*. And that's the problem.

The Hongkong and Shanghai Banking Corporation was not only a key tool of the British Empire in horrors such as the Opium Wars against China, but is in the center of the murderous drug pandemic today.

The point is, we have the resources under our Constitution or the intention of our Constitution, which can meet the challenge of this problem. We have to do it. The only way it's going to happen really is through the role of China and Russia and a few other places like that. Otherwise, you've got nothing coming. But if we can get the cooperation of China and Russia and a few other places which do have some independence, we could do just fine. [applause]

LaRouche's Closing Remarks

LaRouche: OK. First thing, shut down Wall Street. Absolutely shut it down. Don't bring it back. Don't let the wind blow from that direction because it's putrid. All we have to do is to understand these kinds of principles. We know them, I've known them, they're there. But people feel they have to be obedient to government. The problem is the government is not the government. The government is not really the government. They have some fakers who are stand-ins in the name of being the government. But they don't govern for the nation. They govern for the rich!

They steal!

If you want to speak honestly, the way they live is they steal. And the people concede to allow the stealing. And that's all there is. There's no productivity; if you look at the reality of the condition of the citizen in the United States, you have a *falling rate* of the conditions of existence of the citizens in the United States! They're being raped! Everything is being stolen from them that's worth anything.

And somebody comes out and says, "Oh, we've got this, we've got this option, we've got this option." None of it is true.

All we have to do is turn the authority of the United States back to the people of the United States, but according to the kinds of principles which validated the development of the United States and of other nations as well. China and Russia are the leading nations of the world today. Understand that.

See it. Appreciate it. It's the truth. And just understand that.

China has become again a very great nation. It has not reached the full maturity of which it is capable. But China is the first nation now to deal with nearby space. That's where the space program develops. Now this is a modest venture in space but it's going to grow.

Putin's history was that he was a member of a family which died fighting to save the Russia! So Putin is there, he's real, he's honest, he's effective. China is tied closely to Putin now in collaboration and there's something emerging: What is it? There's a change.

Suddenly, the United States doesn't mean much. Why doesn't it mean much? It no longer does anything very useful. It's a bunch of silly fools giving off bad odors. There's nothing good there.

We have to realize we have to change that. We have to understand what the United States was supposed to mean, as Alexander Hamilton provided the guidance. And we have to get the people of the United States to revolt in a certain way, that is to say: *We don't take this crap no more.*

That's all you have to do. And get the people who are going to be running the institutions of government in the United States, let them operate as appropriate members of government. *Shut down Wall Street, bring the British royal family down.* And solve the problems! Stop giving way to slavery! Stop being a slave for the British Empire. Stop killing people around the world for the sake of the British Empire. It's that simple. But it takes the guts required to recognize that that is your mission. And that's the important thing, the recognition of one's *mission* in life *for mankind*, the meaning of the mission of life for mankind.

Once you have that securely fixed, you should be able to do something better than we've been seeing recently.

The British Empire Unleashes The Four Horsemen

This is an edited transcript of Gerry Rose in Dialogue with the Manhattan Project on Saturday, Jan. 9.

Dennis Speed: My name is Dennis Speed, and on behalf of the LaRouche Political Action Committee, I want to welcome everyone here to our second dialogue of the new year of 2016 with Lyndon LaRouche. We don't have Mr. La-Rouche here today; representing Mr. LaRouche will be Gerry Rose from our National Center, and he'll be opening with a statement here in a moment. I just want to let people know that two New York House of Representatives members have requested that the "28 pages" of the famous report of Senator Graham be released. They are Congressman Rangel and Congressman Jeffries.

This is particularly meaningful because, as you know, for the past three weeks in particular, Mr. LaRouche has been making a very emphatic point about the relationship between the release of the "28 pages," the taking down of Barack Obama, and the securing of the

The Four Horsemen of the Apocalypse, a woodcut by Albrecht Dürer from 1498.

United States by means of getting rid of a set of treasonous Presidents, or representatives of the Presidency, including, of course, George W. Bush and Barack Obama.

So, with that, I'm going to introduce Gerry, who'll do an opening statement, and then, as always, we'll go right to questions and answers. So, Gerry?

Gerry Rose: For those of you who've been following the developments as Lyndon LaRouche had forecasted, he warned point-blank, over the last two weeks in December, of the dire consequences of not solving the fundamental question of the total reorganization of the completely bankrupt trans-Atlantic system; he warned in the most dire terms imaginable. You can look at the record; it's there.

And, right on cue, you have had at least a 700-, 800-point drop in the stock market. But more significant is the absolute collapse of the banking systems in Western Europe and the United States. We are on the verge of the complete dissolution, as La-Rouche had warned, of the banking system.

Now, good riddance on some level, because it's so completely, thoroughly rotten, where there were no actual investments in the real economy. As more money was pumped into the banking system, the percentage of real investment got less and less and less. And, as we warned, this "bail-in"—even the whiff of a "bail-in"—which actually occurred in several banks in Italy, has completely panicked any investments, even in the banks. No one in his right mind would invest in the stocks of these banks, and no one has.

So forget about your agendas, forget about what you have projected into the future—it's gone! It is gone; you're living in a world that is precisely defined: If you do not solve the immediate crisis before us, then there will be no future.

What Is a Dark Age?

We're not saying "there's no future," but it's the moment of truth.

I want to just give a little insight that I've been working on; I've had a bit of a sickness for a while, the last six months, and I've been able to think about certain things, and look at them in a certain deep way. And I've studied in great detail what was called the Dark Age of the century of the 1300s to the 1400s.

The Dark Age itself, the actual Black Plague, occurred from 1348 to 1350, in which literally one-third to two-thirds—you know, they didn't have a census at that point—but at least one-third to two-thirds of the population of Europe was completely wiped out by the Plague itself.

And it's very reminiscent of the Four Horsemen of the Apocalypse; all of you have heard about that. But, as you think about it, what are we really facing here? It's war, famine, disease, and, what everybody forgets, death.

Now, that would seem redundant, but it's not. It's not because the Four Horsemen of the Apocalypse come all at once; they don't come in a sequence: First, you get disease, then you get famine, then you get war, then you get death. It doesn't occur that way.

Look at the reality of what we're facing. The commitment of the British Empire to the depopulation of this planet: the open, explicit commitment of Obama to war; you remember the outbreaks of the ebola crisis, and other kinds of things. We are on a precipice.

That doesn't mean we can't solve it, but it means that if you're thinking about what your future will be, if we don't solve this, I can tell you. I've studied it. There's no question about it: You will get a combination of war, famine, disease, and death. That's the reality of the situation. We're not trying to be apocalyptic, but the crisis is of an apocalyptic nature!

And therefore, we must eliminate the combination of factors which are causing this threat: By solving the banking system crisis with a total bankruptcy reorganization around Glass-Steagall we can bring down Wall Street, and bring down the British Empire, which runs Obama.

They are all committed to depopulating this planet.

And finally, the actual genius of this century, one of the most extraordinary geniuses—Lyn doesn't talk about it, because he's the one who's usually here, and he doesn't talk about it. But we have on this planet, in this country, *the* greatest genius of this century. And there have only been two: Albert Einstein, and him. He wouldn't say that. He's extremely humble, but he is.

We actually have presented, in the most profound, clear way in the history of mankind—and I've studied it, so I speak with a certain authority here—what the actual solutions are to this crisis. But not just solutions as formal, programmatic things, but with the fighting will of Joan of Arc in facing this crisis, to actually bring down the enemy of mankind. So, with that, I open it up for questions.

Question: Hi, Gerry. Hello to everyone listening. Start with what I tuned into last night's webcast; I caught most of it, especially Megan Beets; I missed the early part of Jeff Steinberg's presentation. But, how do you deal with everything Jeff had to say? And then, here comes Megan. And so that was very useful to help me to continue to make that connection. That can be easily severed, and I'll tell you why.

In our work around Congress, I had mentioned that one of the junior staff, or administrative assistants, was present at a presentation that we gave; it was very thorough, ran for about 35 minutes. And, afterwards, we engaged one of the assistants in the hallway and invited her to the chorus.

And, indeed, this past Thursday, a number of new people,—I don't know the exact number, but a striking number,—came to the chorus rehearsal for the first time. She was late, but she came and got to observe some things, and at least got an idea, some sense of what was going on, in particular by John's Sigerson] comments. And, afterwards in conversation, we greeted one another, but she was having discussions; one of the members invited her and a boyfriend to this Saturday meeting.

And frankly, I freaked out. I said "Oh, wait! This was a Congressional representative!" I broke exactly that relationship that Jeff and Megan were establishing. I panicked. I said, "No, we won't do the music; we'll do that later!"

Of course, it's so silly, and I'd realized it about a half hour later. But that's what happened.

And so, it's easy to say, "I have the Manhattan Project down pat," until something happens, and then you realize you don't. So, that was the right thing to do, and we need to do that. And, as we move into the next round—now we're doing these e-mails and tracking people down in Congress here, and we'll meet about that after this meeting here. It's something that just struck me about how I needed that webcast, and to break through those fears. Because I literally was like, "Uh no! That's wrong!"

No, that's exactly the right thing to do, and the only way out, is to invite people to get better.

Genius and Courage

Rose: I've always appreciated your insights, because they come from an examination of the fear factors we're up against. Because they are subjective.

We tend to hold on to an idea that somehow "there's going to be a future." We do. We say, "Okay, what's my fallback option?" That's what everybody does. "And, so therefore, let's save something for the future."

The real question on the table is, we have to *create* the future.

I reference this Joan of Arc question, because, France—for 100 years—had no leaders for one hundred years. Now Barbara Tuchman made a mistake when she said: Well, it got so bad, it finally got good. No, it got worse, and worse, and worse. You couldn't imagine—it just got worse! The whole century got worse. As bad as the Black Death was, the wars that ensued, and the locust phenomenon of these marauding armies, just looting everything like locusts! *It was a disaster!*

LaRouche PAC TV

Lyndon LaRouche returned to the National Press Club on Nov. 2, 2012 in an EIR press conference entitled "Benghazi 9/11: Obama's Impeachable Crimes."

It took the Maid of Orleans, as Schiller identifies, with the actual quality of courage. You see, genius has a quality of courage to it. You cannot be a genius, if you're not prepared to risk the hatred, the fear, of everyone around you.

Joan of Arc was a 14-year-old woman who said, "I will save France." And she did. There was *no doubt* in her mind that her mission, no matter what, was to *save her nation* from the locusts that had taken it over. They couldn't even appoint their own King! It was a British king; the British have been bad for a long time, by the way.

And what you're reflecting, which I've always appreciated, is these fear factors; this is why Lyn is so hard on his membership,—you may have noticed that. Why is he so hard on his membership? Because it's precisely the quality of courage that defines genius, real genius.

Albert Einstein was surrounded at the Solvay Conference. And everybody was saying, "You can't prove this!" And he said, "I can, and I'm right." He was surrounded by the scientific establishment of all of Europe, and he never gave an inch.

LaRouche is surrounded by unbelievable fear at best, and the British Empire at worst. And, as you know, he has never once succumbed to these kinds of personal fear factors. Never once. It's extraordinary. And that's why we have an option now to actually solve the problem.

Ironically, the only reason the King of France, the Dauphin, listened to this 14-year-old woman who said, "I can save you," is because there were no other options. And right now, the Congress has no options: We're the only option they've got.

And because we're clear, it's this question of a "certain trumpet." We have sounded, because of Lyn, a "certain trumpet;" it couldn't be more certain. We have to just keep absolutely sounding that louder and clearer; and as the options are gone, and the actual courage of a leadership body that we have represented,—it's not just leadership out of courage. We know what we're doing, and in fact, most of the world—China knows. I had some interesting meetings with Chinese-Americans, and they know we're right; most of the Congress knows we're right. Most of the military who are not insane, know we're right.

But I appreciate that you always raise the right question—and if people would be a little self-reflexive when they flinch—I think you've raised the right question. . . .

How Are We Going to Do This?

Question: I feel as if I'm in the beginning of a novel. I was minding my own business Monday, and—are you the guy I met Monday in Staten Island?

Anyway, Ben Carson came to Staten Island. And I tend to cultivate as many friends as far from me on the political spectrum as I can, and I knew a lot of them would be there. And I hung out. I didn't go up to talk to Carson at the end, although a good friend of mine did. You may have seen her; her video went viral. Rose Uscianowski; she got up to Ben Carson and said, "So you think I chose to be gay?" And that went back and forth for a minute or so, and then finally she said— she's just the sweetest person, and she delivered it perfectly. She goes, "I think you're full of shit." [laughter] That's viral. You should check that out. She's been getting interviews, she's been on the front page of the paper.

Anyway. I'm stalling here because I've heard so many things. I looked at a few more LaRouche videos and this and that, this week. I certainly appreciate the study of the past, to explain what's going on now. I think it's impossible to understand anything, otherwise.

I retired four or five years ago. I started figuring out—well, even before I was retired, in the meltdown, I said, I'm going to try and figure this out. And the first thing I read was about credit default swaps, and I said, "Oops, there they go again"—some other new name. What could this be? And you read and read and—. (sighs)

OK, so here's a question. OK, now when you say the "British Empire" at this point, how many people do you think we're talking about who are running the show? You know, I've been trying to figure this out from the bottom up, and I keep saying, "Well, OK, yeah, this is already pretty bad, but I don't think he's calling the shots. And this guy's not calling the shots. And it's not Congress." And then it kind of dawned on me that it's not even Jamie Dimon, or whatever.

So, how many people are there? And then, evidently, the world as we know it, is going to end next week or something [laughs], is what we're saying here now. Are we just riding this out? Is there anything to do right now? And I love the idea Lyndon LaRouche talks about, "OK, you've got to know the enemy," which I understand completely; I mean because what's the use of fighting this, if the enemy's over there. So many of the people I talk to are on the other side of the political spectrum. They always want to blame the government. And that dawned on me a while ago. Well, *they're* not running the show, so don't blame them.

All right, so the question is, how many people are we fighting? And how are we going to do this?

Rose: That's a good question. First of all, in the words of Percy Bysshe Shelley, "We are many, they are few." Because their power doesn't come from their numbers. Their power doesn't even come from their money.

I'm going to shock you here. You know where their power comes from? From the fact that the majority of the people since the turn of the Twentieth Century have not been given a scientific education. And that was very conscious on the British part.

Bertrand Russell, who was one of the most evil men of the Twentieth Century, created a system of pure logic, so that you could not know *anything—anything*—for sure. You can guess. You can set up tautologies. You can set up logical relations, but you don't know if they are true. In fact, they're not true, by the way. But that's all you can *actually* know.

This goes back to Aristotle, in fact. When the *actual* creators of Western civilization *rejected logic*, they understood something very fundamental. Nicolaus of

Cusa—of course, you've never heard of him, I'm sure of it—who was the actual founder of modern civilization. And what he absolutely, fundamentally attacked, was the idea that logic tells you anything. Because logic is tied to your senses, the way that you interrelate with things. And you make up constructs.

As opposed to the fact that *there is in the Universe itself*, which Vladimir Vernadsky proved conclusively, there is a creative principle; that the Biosphere itself is an actual emanation from something higher.

Life itself is not a logical phenomenon. You cannot describe anything real from logic. There is a higher principle: That principle is what human beings can uniquely access. And as we uniquely access this, we actually create higher energy flux densities by accessing these higher principles; higher energy flux densities, such that we can solve the problems of increased population, the problems of poverty, the problems of lack of sanitation, the problems of infrastructure, things that we need to solve.

Education doesn't come from logic! This comes from a commitment to the future of mankind. And we as individuals have unique capabilities, absolutely unique capabilities, which the British *hate—they're fearful of it.*

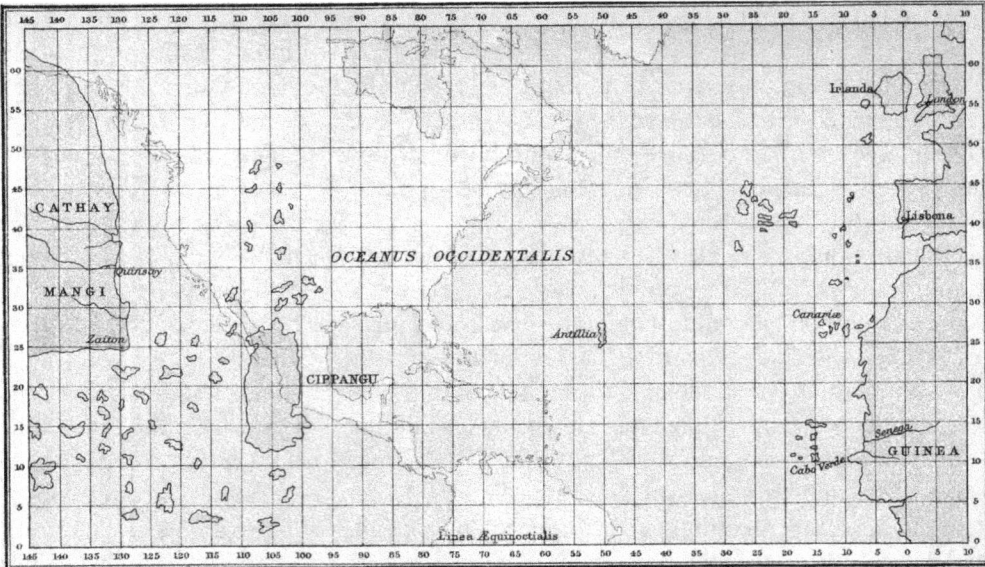

Toscanelli's map, produced in 1474. The correct outline of North America is shown in light blue tint.

A portrait of a man said to be Christopher Columbus, by Sebastiano del Piombo.

The Columbus Principle

That leads to the importance of the culture question. So, in the words of Schiller, we have "to dare to be wise." And our movement is unleashing—particularly in this Manhattan area—that quality of mind, the excitement to be human, the excitement for a future.

I'll tell you something that was really exciting for me yesterday. I had a meeting yesterday with Lynn Yen, who's the head of a group called the Foundation for the Revival of Classical Culture. And she means it, by the way. This is not just a word. So she was taking these young violinists, very talented, young violinists—and you can make comments that they play too fast—and a very young pianist—18 years old. And she was touring them through the Bronx, I believe, or Brooklyn, whatever, to play for these 11 year-olds and 12 year-olds. And they were on fire! "You mean I can do this? You mean I can actually do this kind of thing?

What the hell am I doing with this other stuff?" [Laughs]

So, as humans, we will respond. But you need a human leadership group, which we are, to give people access to that quality of humanity.

I tell you, they're not that bright, our enemies. They're not that bright, and they're not that many! Let me just say it. The Chinese leadership has 1.6-1.7 billion at this point. But what we need in the United States and the trans-Atlantic system is a leadership that is prepared to give people access to this quality of humanity. That's my answer.

Question: [Elliott Greenspan] Yes, my intelligence sources tell me, Gerry, that you were preparing an *EIR* article on what you call "the Columbus Principle." Could you give us a preview of that, some conception of what you're working on? And how that relates to what LaRouche has been emphasizing, the attack on the Renaissance, etc. in the second half of the Fifteenth Century, in that period?

Rose: In fact, what inspired me to think about this, was a question that was asked here in the New York meeting. And I think Roger was the one who asked the question, and LaRouche said, "But you forgot about the Columbus Principle." And this was a complete discontinuity, as you know; you've been to these meetings; he introduced a complete discontinuity.

And most people think, or have been told, that the Renaissance is some,—you know, in the survey courses which I've had, it's always about art and—Italian art, really. And in fact, I've taken the period from Joan of Arc to Columbus, and what I've done and established—which Lyn has said, but I've actually documented it—is that there was a total upheaval in the previous system of thought. It was not just Nicholas of Cusa, who really is a seminal figure. What he did with what's called logic, and Aristotelianism, was a complete—

Can you imagine? He was a cardinal in the Catholic Church, and a very prominent cardinal in the Catholic Church. Now I've read at least 1,100 pages of his, out of 1,400; I've 300 more to go. And these are different dialogues, 20, 30, 40 dialogues. He didn't mention the word "sin" once! This is a Catholic cardinal, who writes 1,100 pages, and he doesn't mention the word "sin."

What he establishes, really—in the most extraordinary depth in history—is that to access your human identity is not to *negate* sin, but that you can overcome sin, become perfect in some sense, if you understand that impulse which comes from the Universe itself. The impulse to be human, to be creative, comes from the Universe itself, and he defines—at least over 1,100 pages, and I'm sure it gets better,—I've got 300 pages more to go, and I'm sure it gets better; but what he defines, which is what I'm going to go through at some point, is, since you cannot directly cognize the Universe, you can't directly get outside the Universe and see it; you can't do that. Otherwise, it wouldn't be the Universe, for instance.

What you can do through the concept of metaphor, which is fundamental to Classical art, is develop the imagination, as our friend said here. The development of imagination is the development of the capacity to understand that which is, as he said, "ineffable." In other words, you can't say it, but you can evoke it. You can evoke a power of what we call "imagination" to define the future, which was not embedded in the logic in the lower levels of thinking.

And by evoking that, Cusa creates, as does Kepler, as does Leonardo da Vinci, and even before there were intimations of that with Brunelleschi and others, but he redefines the whole question; there was the greatest effluence of *genius, in the history of mankind, in every sector.* Including—and this is where the shocker lies in what I will define—including three nation-states which evolve from this idea of man: Louis XI of France, and he was inspired by Jeanne d'Arc; Henry VII of England. Then, around Leonardo da Vinci, Machiavelli, and Amerigo Vespucci. Paolo Toscanelli, they launched a project to get off the European continent because it is too corrupt, to find a new continent. And they actually had the maps to do it! And they gave it to Columbus.

And therefore, this continent was a project, or the Columbus principle was a project, of the explosion of genius. We found this continent, and the implications, when Columbus actually landed in a New World, and proved that everybody's idea of the planet was wrong,—everybody's idea was wrong! The excitement of discovery created navigation, created new ships, created a whole new way of thinking about the Universe and man. And "it had legs," as they say; it had real staying power. Because it was real.

Columbus discovered it, created it. and it's an amazing story, really. So that's what I intend to do with this project.

II. We Need a Renaissance

Is Beauty
A Political Necessity?

The following discussion between Helga Zepp-LaRouche, founder of the Schiller Institutes, and Megan Beets of LaRouche PAC was recorded Jan. 13 on LaRouche PAC's New Paradigm for Mankind program. For video of the program, go to this page.

Beets: We are situated in an extremely ominous global strategic situation. The global financial system has now entered fully the final collapse phase, and without the without the protection of the Franklin Roosevelt Glass-Steagall Act, we're looking at a complete expropriation of the population's savings, and rising death rates. We've already seen this happen in the case of Greece, and places around the United States. And this is what you and your husband have warned about. Unless we get an entirely new system, the world is looking at a collapse phase into a New Dark Age.

Now this is going hand-in-hand with a real escalation in the war danger, and we've seen this in the rising provocations against China, with what happened in the situation around North Korea just this week. And the world situation has really escalated to a point of dramatic decision. We have to decide in the next hours and days, which direction the world wants to go in.

And as you and your husband have both said, there's no *practical* way out of this crisis. Mr. LaRouche has said many times that only shutting down the British Empire can save humanity. And you, yourself, have said many times, put it this way, that mankind has to decide to break with the current system, and usher in a complete New Paradigm, based upon completely new principles.

I think that the general population is getting a stronger and stronger sense of this, that mankind cannot continue down the pathway that we've been on, up till now, and that something new is needed.

However, I think that people often have a very difficult time even beginning to think about what that new system could be, what it could, or should, be like. And that, I think, is really what I would like to discuss with you today. What are the principles that are powerful enough to carry mankind into a beautiful new future?

The Crucial Ideas of Friedrich Schiller

For that, I think the ideas of Friedrich Schiller are crucial, especially for our American audience, to whom he is almost completely unknown. So Schiller is somebody whom you have been intimately familiar with since you were very young, and he's somebody upon whose ideas you've based a lot of your own thinking, and a lot of your very important and successful political work over the past decades. So that's why I invited you here today, and what I would like to open up a discussion about.

Just to say a few things to situate Schiller for our audience. Friedrich Schiller was born in 1759 in Germany, very close to Stuttgart. He died in 1805 at a young age, in Weimar, Germany. Many people might be familiar with Schiller, if only from his great poem, *An Die Freude (The Ode to Joy),* which Beethoven famously set in his Ninth Symphony. But Schiller was not just a poet, and I think we'll get into this. He was also a great dramatist, a great historian, a great philosophical thinker, and a great, as you put it, psychologist.

What I find most striking, throughout all of his works, is Schiller's complete commitment to the idea that it's not only possible, but necessary, to create a society which is moral, just, and good, and to move mankind into his adulthood. So, if we think of today's insane Dark Age vs. Renaissance state of warfare as perhaps the throes of pu-

Helga Zepp-LaRouche at the founding conference of the Schiller Institute on July 3, 1984. To her left is Lyndon LaRouche and the Institute's Musical Director, John Sigerson.

berty of mankind, it is possible for mankind to put that state behind him and move into his adulthood.

But this idea, I think, for people living, especially in the Trans-Atlantic area, is so far removed from what they see around them, that it's difficult to grasp that this is even possible.

How Can We Get Out of This Dark Age

Zepp-LaRouche: Well, I think, from my standpoint, the image of man which Friedrich Schiller developed in the most beautiful way—I don't know any thinker, internationally, in any culture, who has designed a more beautiful image of what man can be. And given the fact that we are living in a Dark Age, as you've just correctly mentioned, where barbarism and degeneracy is prevalent, I think he is probably the most immediately needed antidote to that.

Because, when the French Revolution failed in Europe, in the time of Schiller, you had had the American Revolution, and that was what all great republicans were looking towards. They were hoping that they could overturn the oligarchical system in Europe, and replace it with one modeled on the American Revolution.

The beginning of the French Revolution was hope-fully going in this direction, but then when the Jacobin terror took over, that hope vanished. And at that point Schiller wrote the *Aesthetical Letters*, because he said, "How could it be that such a pregnant moment, such a moment full of opportunity, failed?" And he developed the idea of an aesthetical education of man, because he said, "This great moment had found a little people." The objective condition for political change was there, but the subjective moral condition was lacking, and therefore, he said, "From now on, all improvement in politics must come through the ennoblement of the individual."

And that is one of my deepest convictions for today: that if you don't make people better people, then there is no way you can improve the political situation. Because you can have different democratic arrangements, different coalitions, but if the people become worse,—and they're becoming worse right now,—then the vector of development goes downhill. So Schiller then, in these *Aesthetical Letters*, said, "But where should the improvement of people come from, when the governments are corrupt?" That's for sure a condition we have today. He added, "and if the masses are degenerate and depraved"; that's also a condition we have today.

Classical Art for People To Ennoble Themselves

So he then came to the very surprising answer—for some people surprising,—that the only way you can get better people, to get them to ennoble themselves, is through great Classical Art. And that is exactly the conclusion we have come to: that if you do not appeal to that higher identity in the human mind, which each human being is capable of having, you can't succeed.

That was another idea of Schiller. He said, "Each person has an ideal person inside him, and it is the great task of his existence, or her existence, to fulfill that great potential, and make that ideal person, which potentially is inside everybody, identical with the real person."

And I find this also a very beautiful answer to the idea of, Why are we here? Why are we on the planet Earth? What is the purpose of our existence? And to improve ourselves to become as close as possible to that ideal person inside ourselves, and use that then, to improve the progression of mankind, in general, which is one of the other goals Schiller set. For example, in the very beautiful writing about the laws of Solon and Lycurgus, he said that the purpose of mankind is progress, which is very simple, but I think …

Beets: But it's very controversial for today.

Zepp-LaRouche: Oh yes. Yes. So I'm as enthusiastic about Schiller as I was when I was a schoolgirl.

The Inalienable Rights of Man

Beets: In 1984, you founded the Schiller Institute, and one of the founding documents was "The Inalienable Rights of Man," which was a very slightly altered version of the American Declaration of Independence. Since that time, with the Schiller Institute you've led tremendous political and cultural work in countries around the world, not only countries in the so-called Western World. So maybe you could just say something about the importance of having based the Schiller Institute and the political work on Schiller, and what that's opened up.

Zepp-LaRouche: Well, the Schiller Institute idea was to found an institute to improve foreign relations, relations among states, because I thought that the condition of international relations was terrible. It's based on subversion, on coups, on interventionism, on all kinds of terrible things. So, I had the idea that the only way you can have a foreign policy which is really adequate to the dignity of man, is to relate to the best tradition of the other country.

In other words, when I'm relating to Americans, I want to relate to Lincoln, or to John Quincy Adams, or some of the great Presidents. When people relate to Germany, I don't want them to reduce history to twelve years of the bottom, but I want them to think of the high points of Cusanus, of Kepler, Leibniz, Schiller, Beethoven—and with all other countries, as well. When I then thought, who would be the best person to give that idea a name? I found that it was Friedrich Schiller. So I think that the very idea of the aesthetical education of man as the absolutely most important ingredient in world politics today, is as relevant now as it was then.

Beets: Could you say more about what is aesthetical education? What does that mean, and is Schiller the only one who's spoken about it?

Overcoming Aristotle

Zepp-LaRouche: That is not quite true. The idea of an aesthetical education developed slowly. It was actually an answer to Aristotle, really, because Aristotle said the actor should get on the stage and act out his feelings. When he plays an angry person, he should be angry. When he plays a sad person, he should be sad. The school of rhetoric developed out of that, and they said it doesn't have to be true, it just has to be convincing.

If you look at politics today,—I don't want to name certain Presidential candidates in the United States, but they do this. They activate this big emotional hype—and people fall for it. How do you employ rhetoric to appeal to the senses of the audience? But it doesn't have to be truthful.

Aesthetical education was really the opposite. It said, you have to develop the inner person, you have to develop the inner-directedness of the freedom of the soul. You have to educate people to become beautiful souls.

When I was a young woman, or girl, in school, I was really mesmerized by this idea of a beautiful soul. Because I looked around and I said, all these girls are concerned about how they look; how much make-up, or not, they should use; or the boys, how big biceps they should have, and what not. But who cares about the beauty of their soul?

Schiller had the idea that you can educate not only your mind, your intellect, but that you can, through beauty, educate your emotions. So eventually, when you reach the goal, or the proximity of a beautiful soul, you can blindly trust your emotions, because they will never tell you anything different than what reason would command. His definition of a beautiful soul was, that it's a person for whom freedom and necessity, duty and passion, are the same thing. And then later he said, the only person for whom this condition applies is the genius. However, he said everybody can become a genius. That is what beauty really is.

Republican vs. Oligarchical

That came from his very deep anti-oligarchical conviction. To my knowledge, he was probably one of the first people, if not the first person, in general, who differentiated between the oligarchical system, and the republican system.

I have mentioned his writings about Solon and Lycurgus, where he described Solon, the state model based on natural law, on the common interest of man, as the focus of mankind, as compared to Sparta, the oligarchical model, where you have a small elite subjugating the masses. He had this idea that if every human being becomes a beautiful soul, or becomes a genius, then oligarchy will vanish, because then people are self-thinking and inner-directed.

That, by the way, is what is lacking the most today. People have completely forgotten to be self-governed, self-thinking, the inner freedom is not... People complain about all kinds of external tyrannies, and dictatorships, and so forth, but I think the biggest tyranny is the inability to be inner-directed. As I said, I don't know anybody who is so much concerned with that, the idea of the inner freedom. And he defines beauty as the freedom in appearance, and I think that this is so important for today.

Beets: Can you say more about that, the freedom in appearance?

Zepp-LaRouche: He had an idea of beauty which was very much detached from sensuous experience. He said there must be a condition of beauty which is basi-

Joan of Arc (1412-1431) depicted on horseback in an illustration from a 1505 manuscript. She was one of Schiller's exemplars of a "beautiful soul."

cally an idea based on reason. And it's not like what the English Enlightenment would say, that an idea comes from the distillation of sensuous experience. The English Enlightenment, they basically had this idea, man is born as a *tabula rasa* [blank slate], and then you bang your head against the wall, which is an experience, and then you make an idea out of that, which is sort of ridiculous.

So Schiller said, no, there must be an *idea* of beauty, so that when you find something beautiful in reality, and it coincides, that is a lucky coincidence, but that does not mean that this idea of beauty comes from the sensuous experience. And that idea of harmonious development, the idea of freedom in the appearance, is exactly what corresponds.

Because you see, Kant was very prevalent in the 1790s, which was when Schiller wrote many of these aesthetical writings. Kant had the idea that you have to have a Law of Morality, the so-called categorical imperative, that you should not do anything you don't want to be done to you, to yourself, and that you sort of have to have rules, which you obey.

Overcoming the Brutalization of the Population

And Schiller was very upset. He said, we who love freedom so much, don't even want to look at the procedure by which a person forces himself to be moral,—aghh! I have to be moral. The people go to church, and they say, I have to be moral, and then on Monday, they behave as piggishly as on Saturday.

But he said that basically it is the inner conviction which should guide you. And beauty is both sensuous,—it obviously pleases the senses,—but it is also an emotion born out of reason. So beauty helps you to educate your emotion, and he had the idea that Art which is not beautiful, should not be called Art, because it's not Art. Only if it's beautiful, does it elevate people. And I agree with that. That's also not the popular view today, but I fundamentally agree with it.

Beets: Right. It's very much against the popular view, but I think it does get to something I was thinking about. What you're saying, and Schiller is saying, is that everyone in society can aspire to, and achieve, the level of genius, and that within everyone there's the potential that his impulses would be coherent with the good, and with reason. I think that seems such an impossible idea, when you look around in society today, but I think what you're bringing up about Art, and culture generally, which is something which is a social thing.... It is something which is shared as an identity among an entire culture and an entire people, and gives a sense of the pathway by which you could educate masses of people to that level.

Zepp-LaRouche: I think that great Art is really very, very important, because you have today a culture which is going from ugly to more ugly, and every time you think the bottom has been reached, some perverse satanist comes up with something worse.

I think that that is really deliberate. It's part of an

clipart.com
The descent of the French Revolution into barbarism like this, is what inspired Schiller to write his Aesthetical Letters.

oligarchical system. You had it in the Roman Empire with the circus and the amphitheater, where the Christians were thrown to the lions, or the gladiators were fighting, and then the audience was asked by the Emperor, should this person live, or die, and the person could make thumbs up or thumbs down, determining if the person would be killed. And they did that deliberately to engage the population in brutalization, because by participating in such a murder, which it *de facto* was, you would make people worse, and controllable.

On the other side, in great Classical Art,—in music it's very much obvious, but also in great poetry, in painting, in architecture, in city-building, in practically every art form,—what you do is you appeal to that faculty of the human mind where creativity is located. So that is why great scientists always—I don't know any exception—were also playing music, listening to music, and it would increase their ability to form hypotheses.

Because creativity is when you have to think about something that did not exist before. So you have to put your mind in that sort of playful condition, where you are willing to think something which does not exist in the existing body of knowledge. If you follow the great compositions in music, or you study great Classical drama, or you look at a poem, Classical poems, not just Dadaism, or some arbitrary phrases,—great Classical poetry is extremely important.

Think about what the difference is between prose and the poem. The meaning of the poem does not lie in the prose, and it forces your mind to form that higher level of idea, which is this intangible, this thing which has no weight, no dimension, but is effective. Ideas are the most effective thing in the universe. And great Art is what makes the mind able to think these beautiful things called ideas.

Beets: I was just reading Humboldt's account of the development of Schiller's mind, and he talks about that moment in the poem when you can't reason the meaning out of the words anymore. The only thing that's left is for the imagination to make a leap, a powerful leap of hypothesis to exactly this new concept that you're discussing. Only poetry and art can do such a thing.

Zepp-LaRouche: Yes.

Empfindungsvermögen

Beets: Let me ask you this then, because in the *Aesthetical Letters*, Schiller has a concept which is not in the English language in the same way, but the German word is *Empfindungsvermögen*. There are many ways to translate it. One is the capacity for feeling, or the capacity to be moved by emotion, maybe. But he said that that is the thing which is the most lacking in the culture. Truth in the culture is not going to come from any more knowledge or information. It has to be found in the *Empfindungsvermögen*. So I wonder, if you could enlighten Americans more on this concept.

Zepp-LaRouche: Schiller also said at one other point that most people in the modern times,—that was 200 years ago—are like crippled plants. If you've ever tried to garden, you probably know that if you put too much light, then the plants become long and thin. If you put too much fertilizer, they die. If they have too much water, or too little water...

So a crippled plant is a person who has developed maybe one aspect of his potential personality, but has no harmonious development. What is lacking, therefore,—people may have skills in an area, they may be good engineers, or they may be good scientists, or maybe good at whatever they are, but they are not capable of absorbing the totality of the world into their own being, let alone the universe.

What Schiller basically said is, it is that quality which—I have struggled to find a good English expression, and the closest I came was many words, not one word. I would call it the totality of the ability of the mind and the soul to absorb the world. And he said that the development of that quality is the most important necessity of his time. And if he were around today, he would say, oh, my God, it's so much more important today.

And therefore, I think that the idea of developing that quality is really a challenge for us today. In a certain sense this was already expressed by Gotthold Lessing, who was a generation earlier, preparing the German Classical period. In his writings on aesthetical education, he said that the most important quality is compassion, which is sort of going in the same direction. And he said, people should listen and look at great Classical drama, because in the drama, you can train your emotions, because you can feel larger issues than are in your immediate environment.

Schiller wrote a beautiful essay about the theater as a moral institution. He said if a normal person, a baker, or a hair-dresser, goes into a theater, and sees the great fate of mankind on the stage, and if the drama is well written, he or she has to identify with the person on the stage, and that way become bigger than in his or her real life. And that way you can train in a playful way, the kind of emotions you really need in your own life, day to day. I think that that is something we really have to go back to. Because that's why you have to go to the high points in culture, when you try to get out of the present decay.

That is really why we should concern ourselves with all of these people, Schiller, Lessing, and others. Because the big question is, how do we mobilize in humanity right now that inner force to get us from the abyss,—and we are clearly at the abyss. Now we're at the verge of nuclear war. We are in the middle of a new financial crash, and people are not prepared.

Everybody a King

And it may look like a deviation, or like a diversion, to then say that we have to look at great Classical Art. We have to read Schiller's play *Wilhelm Tell*. *Wilhelm Tell* is very important, because there is this famous Rütli Oath, which expresses the commitment of the Swiss people, at that time, which is almost identical with the text of the Declaration of Independence; or *Don Carlos*, where in the famous scene between Philip II and the Marquis of Posa, the Marquis of Posa says to Philip, "be a king of a million kings"; don't be a king lording over your underlings, but let everybody be a king.

And I find this a beautiful idea. Everybody should be a king. Everybody should be on the highest level of their humanity. You go back to these dramas, and you find there the concepts, which get you out of the present low conception of man.

I think it's very important that we have a Renaissance movement where people really go back to the highest levels. Because every Renaissance which ever happened in the history of mankind, was possible because people would go to the highest expression of culture of the previous period, and then sort of bathing in that, absorbing it, and then creating something new. That's what we have to do today.

Beets: That brings me to something I want to ask you to elaborate more, which is on the role of the artist.

I think you've touched on it in different ways, but Schiller had a very particular idea of the role and the identity of the artist in society. And you see it echoed in other people. Percy Shelley wrote a very famous essay, called, *In Defence of Poetry,* where he said that poets uniquely have the capacity to reflect the shadows of the futurity, and bring them into the present, and therefore poets are the true legislators of the world. And I think you also see it later in a different way in Einstein, who said that the imagination is more

The scene of the Swiss taking the Rütli Oath in 1307, which Schiller featured in his drama Wilhelm Tell*.*

important than knowledge, because it's through the imagination that you come to grasp new things that aren't part of the current world.

I was wonder if you would elaborate more specifically on the role of the artist in this kind of challenge that you've put out?

The Artists

Zepp-LaRouche: Schiller wrote a beautiful poem, which I don't know if it's translated, or if it's well translated. It's called *The Artists*, and it is one of the most beautiful celebrations of how science and art inspire each other, and really lead to the combination of the two leading to this harmonious personality.

He also wrote several theoretical writings about this, one of them being the critique of Gottfried Bürger's poems. Bürger was Schiller's contemporary, and he would write in an absolutely Aristotelian way,—cry out your pain,—and had an terrible conception of what poetry should be. So Schiller used that occasion to again say what the mindset of the artist must be. For example, a poet must dare to move his audience, because, Schiller says, the artist has a unique ability to move the heart, and reach into the innermost movements of the soul. And because he has that power, he must have the highest standard for himself. Schiller demands that the artist ennoble himself to be an ideal man in the moment he performs his art.

Two Forms of Law

William C. Morey

The lawgiver and poet Solon of Athens (640-558)

The lawgiver Lycurgus of Sparta (800-730)

If you think about certain conductors or singers who have really proven they can move people's hearts, you know that they are, at least in the moment of performance,—they are humanity. They express the idea of mankind. That may not be the case all the time. They may go back and have some... I know many people who do excellent music. I have known many of them over the years. And with some, I would hope that they would only do music, because their most beautiful humanity comes out in the moment they do that. And I advised several: Look, why don't you cut the intervals, where you're not like that? And obviously it's a process of perfection.

But I think Schiller demanded that the artist have an absolutely sure knowledge about what his effect, and the effect of his art is on the audience. That has to be a free expression of the audience, but the artist has to be sure about it.

So how do you solve that paradox? He says the selection of what you present must be a universal truth; it cannot be some arbitrary arabesque. This is totally contrary to Kant, who said an arabesque is more beautiful than something where you can see the plan of the Creator. Your creation has to evoke the freedom of the audience. So it has to be universally true, and it has to encourage that inner quality of the audience which makes man truly free.

Schiller was very serious about that. For example, in the preface to his play *The Bride of Messina*, he said that what Art should do is to set us free, not only for a moment, but really. So he says the person who goes to a concert or to a play, who is touched by the power of this performance—when he goes out, that power remains with him.

And I found that to be very true. Because when you look at something horrible, like so-called *Regietheater* art,—this modernist interpretation of the great Classical Art—or even a bad play, it does the same thing with you but in the other direction. I have found that even if it is only for clinical purposes, I look at something ugly, it haunts me for days. I have terrible feelings and emotions and images in my mind, and it's very difficult to get rid of them.

This is why Plato, for example, advised that children should not even look at the plays of the great Greek tragedians, because they would portray murder in the family, revenge, bloody circumstances. And he said that children's minds should not be impressed with such ugliness. Now if Plato, or Schiller, for that matter, would see our modern entertainment, which is all blood and gore, violence, pornography—but mostly violence—they would say, how can children have a chance to become true human beings, if their minds are already molested at an early age by this horrible entertainment?

So I think that therefore, Art has to be exactly on the level which Schiller requires. And I think that it can be done, because on the other side, I think that Schiller also agreed—I don't have any evidence that he knew Nicholas of Cusa, but the same spirits reflects itself in all his writings—that once you taste the sweetness of truth, of beauty and truth, that you do not want other sweetnesses any more. So I believe that once people have access to great Classical Art, and they experience the powerful effect it has on them, they become totally impassioned about it.

Beets: You said something about the process of perfection, and I think you were just referring to it from the standpoint of the individual, the individual artist over time. But also, when we were talking the other day, we discussed it from the standpoint of society as a whole: that Schiller asserts the concept of the ideal, but this is not a fixed goal. This is something which society is constantly able to develop toward. So I was wondering if you could elaborate a little bit more on that.

Zepp-LaRouche: He says, for example, in the *Aesthetical Letters*,—I forget, it was, maybe the 11th letter, or so,— that the goal is the direction, and it has been reached, once you move on it, or once you have chosen it, which sounds paradoxical. But it's true, because Schiller taught many times, in his works, in his poems, in his dramas—they are full of this idea that there is an inner cohesion between the creative human mind, and the lawfulness of the universe.

He even wrote poems about it. For example, he wrote a beautiful poem about Columbus, Columbus crossing the ocean and discovering America. I'm now using my own words, and there is this formulation where he said that what the mind conceptualized, nature had to prove to give. He says it more beautifully than I'm saying it now, but it's the idea that there is something in the human mind which is absolutely in correspondence with the laws of the universe, mentioned yesterday in the Policy Committee discussion; and it is the human mind which drives that force in the universe, your mind being part of the universe, not some observing or something outside of it.

I think that that is what will move mankind forward forever. Schiller was convinced that there is a limitless perfectibility of mankind, and I think that is absolutely true. If you look at history, we only have maybe five

One of the more than a dozen statues of Friedrich Schiller in cities throughout the United States. This one is in Columbus, Ohio.

thousand years of history which has been recorded, through writing, or some other form that is intelligible. I mean, that's just nothing You said that mankind is a teenager. I think we are in an embryonic condition of mankind in terms of what the potential is for mankind to develop.

What Happened to Schiller in America?

Beets: That's a beautiful idea. I hope it's the case.

One final question, at least, for today, or final topic to bring up: Americans today, almost nobody today, knows Schiller, but that wasn't always the case. If you go back to the Nineteenth Century, Schiller was extremely well known. In a lot of our major cities, you have statues of Schiller in the city center somewhere, or in the parks in the middle of the cities. His plays were performed. So, what happened? Why have Americans lost this great thinker?

Zepp-LaRouche: I think, as you said, when there were the celebrations for his hundredth birthday in 1859, or the hundredth anniversary of his day of death in 1905, there were thousands of people who watched the plays in German, in Chicago, in Philadelphia, in many other places. And people really loved Schiller. He was the most beloved German poet ever. And I think one-third of Americans have, according to a census of 2012, German heritage. That's not little. One-third is quite some component of the American identity.

Now that unfortunately got completely eliminated through Teddy Roosevelt, because you had the Anglophile tradition in America of basically the agents of the British Empire, who tried to undo the American Revolution. First was the War of 1812. Then actually the Confederacy was allied with the British Empire, and eventually, when Teddy Roosevelt, and later Woodrow Wilson, moved America to join Great Britain in the First World War against Europe, against Germany, then that radically shifted American culture, because in the Nineteenth Century, you had no professor who had not either studied in Germany under the Humboldt system, or who was not a pupil of somebody who had done so.

So the influence of German Classical culture in the Nineteenth Century in America was huge. But then you had this intervention which really shifted the identity of America, through America entering the First World War on the side of the British, those against whom the American Revolution was made. Then the whole idea of being German was made hateful. People changed their names. They had German names, and they would make them sound Russian, or sound Polish; and with that, unfortunately, and then actually the Second World War, the horror of the Nazis, was the next wave of that.

So therefore, America has been cut off from the most beautiful components of its tradition. That is my view, and America will probably not recover if you don't re-discover that tradition.

Beets: OK. I think that's a great place to end. Do you have anything final you want to say to our audience?

Zepp-LaRouche: No, but I would like people to know—you have published four volumes of translations of Schiller, which are excellent translations. We've had the need to do our own translations, because many translations—to do a good translation, you have to be a poet in two languages. And that is not so easy, but Will Wertz did an excellent job. We have four volumes, so if people really want to start looking into it, well, just write to us, and get these volumes, and I can promise you, you will not be bored.

Beets: Good. Thank you all for watching. We'll put links in the video description to where you can find some of the translations which are available on the Schiller Institute website, as well as order the full volumes of the books, and begin your studies. So, thank all of you for watching. Thank you very much, Helga, and we'll see you soon.

Book Review

Brunelleschi's Tempered Proportions

by Liliana Gorini

Architecture and Music
by Lando Bartoli
Florence, Italy: Edizioni dell'Erba, 1998
42 pages, paperback

Jan 6—In the most recent weeks, Lyndon LaRouche has been emphasizing the importance of Brunelleschi's Dome in Florence for starting a new Renaissance worldwide. A close friend of the LaRouches, Lando Bartoli was the world expert on the dome Brunelleschi designed for the cathedral of Santa Maria del Fiore in Florence.

In the 1980s Bartoli fought alongside the Schiller Institute to save the dome from the risk of destruction, when a proposal was implemented to fill with cement its 48 staging holes, where its edge meets the supporting structure[1] inside the Dome, They had purposely been left open by Brunelleschi. The holes were key to the Dome's construction,—which was a true revolution in architecture at the time of the Italian Renaissance.

Bartoli won this battle, and the Dome of Brunelleschi still stands, in all its beauty, as it has since 1434.

---

1. The story is told in an interview with Bartoli titled, *Can the Dome of Florence Cathedral Be Saved?* in *EIR*, March 25, 1988.

It is the first thing you see when you come to Florence by train.

In 1998, before he passed away in 2002, Bartoli published this little-known booklet, *Architettura e musica*, which echoes what Lyndon LaRouche has been saying through the years about the connection between music and science, and between science and art in general, including, of course, Renaissance architecture.

The book reports on Bartoli's measurements of the Chiesa di San Salvatore al Monte, also in Florence, in order to demonstrate that it was built based on golden mean proportions, as were also the Brunelleschi Dome,

The church of San Salvatore al Monte, cited as an example of musical architecture by Bartoli.

the Pazzi Chapel, and many other churches and chapels of the Italian Renaissance. But Bartoli goes beyond the "criteria of proportions" (harmonic, geometric, and arithmetic) used by Antonio del Pollaiolo in building this church, and investigates their connection to musical intervals.

This connection is something emphasized by both Brunelleschi and Leon Battista Alberti, which recalls Leonardo da Vinci's definition of music as the "representation of the invisible." And it is something which is proven by Brunelleschi's Pazzi Chapel, which is able to "sing back" to a singer since it was built on the basis of the same golden mean proportions as the human, trained, *bel canto* voice.

In order to prove that for the case of the San Salvatore al Monte church in Florence, Bartoli built a lattice "using the Florentine unit of length, the braccio" (0.5836 meters) "inserted into reticular grids which represented the octave, fifth, fourth, whole step, unison, etc., in order to have the demonstration of the perfect formulation of the proportional and harmonic plan of Leon Battista Alberti."

Measuring the nave, sanctuary, and other sides of the church, on this basis, Bartoli came to the following conclusion: "Translating these ratios and numbers into musical terms, you can define the first one (14:14) as a unison, the second one (1:3) as a fifth (analogous to the 2:3 ratio since 1:3 is the octave of 2:3), and the third one (48:54) as a fourth."

Further on in the book he writes: "Nothing could demonstrate better than this, the fact that Renaissance artists did not mean to translate music into architecture, but, in the harmonic intervals of the musical scale, they saw the audible proof of the beauty of the ratios of small whole numbers 1:2:3:4."

The Harmony of Bach

Discussing this matter with an Italian cellist and composer, Pietro Grossi, Bartoli got confirmation of this music-architecture link from the work of the most important Classical composers, including J.S. Bach, "who used to create his musical compositions using reverse motion, mirror fugues and the reverse of the mirrored." This statement reminded me of discussions we

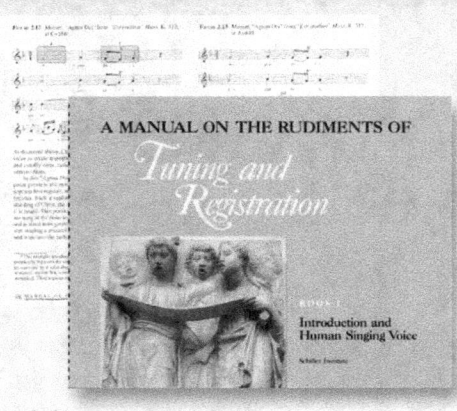

had in the 1970s with Mr. LaRouche on Bach's *Art of the Fugue*, which includes a mirror fugue (or rather two fugues, one of which is the mirror image of the other). It is as though a mirror were placed above or below an existing fugue, producing inversions of each interval in each part, as well as inverting the position of the parts within the texture, so that, for example, the topmost part in one fugue is inverted to produce the lowest part in the other. This is well demonstrated by the two four-part fugues of Contrapunctus 12 in the *Art of the Fugue*.

According to Bartoli, Leon Battista Alberti and Brunelleschi proceeded in the same way as Bach. "Architects have the same possibility, since the same harmonies are kept if we observe an architecture as a whole in front, if we read it from left to right, from right to left, if we admire it bottom up or top down. In a few words, we use both categories, space and time, which in our spirit cancel distinctions which according to our sensitivity in reality never existed."

"As Alberti writes," Bartoli concludes, " 'architects do not use such numbers in a confused or mixed way, but in such a way that they may correspond and allow harmony from all sides.' "

This harmony is the reason why Renaissance buildings still convey to their viewers a sense of lawfulness of the Universe, and beauty, the same lawfulness and beauty which is conveyed to listeners by a composition of Bach, Beethoven, or Giuseppe Verdi.

Bartoli's work is an important first phase in revealing the true nature of Brunelleschi's thought. Brunelleschi's creative work is reflected most strongly in the *non-mathematical* curvature of the Dome in Florence. All of the whole-number proportions that he employed in the beautiful edifices of his design, must necessarily be *tempered*, not "pure" intervals, in the same way that freedom in the musical domain as discovered by J.S. Bach requires that the intervals of the musical scale be tempered, so as to effect a dynamically harmonious whole.

The secret, still waiting to be revealed by future investigators, is exactly *how* Brunelleschi tempered his intervals, in a way which anticipated the great Bernhard Riemann's work by five centuries.

III. Asia Will Not Submit

Launch of AIIB Marks New Paradigm in Economic Governance

by William C. Jones

Jan. 18—The official launch of the much-anticipated Asian Infrastructure Investment Bank (AIIB) in Beijing on Jan. 16 has appeared as a ray of sunshine on an otherwise stormy, and even terrifying, economic and strategic horizon. Since Jan. 1, 2016, the entirety of the London/Wall Street trans-Atlantic financial system has entered into a new phase shift of accelerating and total collapse, just as Lyndon LaRouche warned in the days immediately prior to the recent Christmas season. This collapse has been accompanied both by increasing demands from the British Monarchy for world-wide population reduction accompanied by murderous austerity policies, as well as an escalation by the British Empire, via their puppet Barack Obama, toward a thermo-nuclear war confrontation with Russia and China.

The world sits at the precipice of hell, with London's Specter of Death prepared to unleash global genocide on a scale never before contemplated in human history. It is within this context that the singular launching of the AIIB should be seen—not as the solution to this crisis, but as a transformative initiative which expands the possibility for

Chinese President Xi Jinping addresses the opening ceremony of the AIIB in Beijing on Jan. 16.

breaking the power of London and Wall Street, and aiding in the creation of a new global economic system.

Bail-Ins and Austerity

The ongoing disintegration of the European financial system, a disintegration which is escalating day-by-day, has already resulted in the initiation of the "bail-in policy" at the beginning of this year, a policy which will rob holders of European bank accounts of their savings for the benefit of paying the debts of the speculators and gamblers. Under the bail-in, normal citizens can have their savings and deposits seized—without compensation—and then the stolen funds can be used to pay off the speculative financial debts of the very same banks and financial institutions. This is now the law in Europe, as well as in the United States, under the provisions of the Dodd-Frank Act.

The ravages of the last several years of austerity policies, imposed on the countries of Europe by the London-steered International Monetary Fund, have already brought many of those countries to their knees, resulting in both massive unemployment and drastic cuts in essential services. Now, as a result of the bail-in policy, the citizens of these same nations are in danger of losing their personal savings as well. The death rate in the most devastated countries in the south of Europe has been rising, as well as the suicide rate. And the collapse of the hospital systems portends the spread of new epidemic diseases, as we have seen recently in Brazil with the zika virus.

Similarly in the United States, the Obama policy has led to drastic cuts in public spending on needed infrastructure and services. The death toll in many states hard hit by the depression, like West Virginia, is rising rapidly. Conditions there are now being compared to those that prevailed in the early 1930s before the launch of Roosevelt's New Deal.

The Chinese Initiative

It is in the context of this worsening nightmare that a bright light is beckoning from Asia, largely to be found in the sane economic policies of the nation of China.

Despite the recent "turbulence" in the Chinese financial markets—a turbulence created by errors in judgment from some Chinese leaders who were duped into imitating the West's speculative stock exchange model of finance—the real physical Chinese economy is continuing to grow. China has now become the the most important manufacturing country in the world. To ensure the continuation of this tangible physical economic growth, Chinese leaders are now intent on changing the financial "rules of the game," as these rules have been dictated by the London-New York financial oligarchy up to this time.

This shift in directionality began with the launch in September 2013 by China's new president, Xi Jinping, of the *Silk Road Economic Belt* and the *Twenty-first Century Maritime Silk Road*. These two projects,

The cover of EIR's New Silk Road report, now translated into Chinese. Available for $35 at store.larouchepub.com.

dubbed "The Belt and Road," represent a massive infrastructure investment plan for Central, South and Southeast Asia, which will provide the impetus for developing the economies of these nations and eliminating poverty entirely. China has a proven record in this field, having lifted hundreds of millions of people out of poverty within only two decades.

Hard on the heels of the launch of the Belt and Road, President Xi Jinping, in October 2013, proposed the creation of an Asian Infrastructure Investment Bank, which would bring together the capital of the various nations in the region to assist in that endeavor. While China had significant funds for realizing the Belt and Road itself, the creation of the AIIB transforms this initiative from a "Chinese project" to one of regional cooperation among a broad array of nations. The AIIB brings the countries of the region together, and aids them in financing their own infrastructure and creating a new type of financial structure, one in which the Asian nations, for the first time, become key players.

The initiation of the AIIB gives a clear indication of what direction China wishes to give the world. The AIIB is solely focused on infrastructural investment. Up until now the British Empire-controlled World Bank and Asian Development Bank, together with the International Monetary Fund, have played the dominant role in controlling "infrastructural investment" in Asia. The agenda of these institutions has been nothing short of Imperial genocide and enforced backwardness. They have used their power to stop large scale economic development and, instead, to fund "sustainable" energy projects, social engineering programs, micro-credits for small village co-ops, and population reduction programs.

The AIIB, on the other hand, is to be solely focused on infrastructure investment,—transport, water, and power—the only real long-term solution for reducing world poverty. As Jin Liqun, elected the first president of

Xinhua/Hou Jiansen

Jin Liqun, President of the AIIB, has emphasized that infrastructure development is the key to reducing poverty.

the AIIB, said at his press conference on Jan. 17 following the launch, "Infrastructure is key for broad-based economic development and for poverty reduction."

How the AIIB Will Work

Investment will focus on the development of infrastructure and other productive sectors in Asia, including energy and power, transportation and telecommunications, rural infrastructure and agricultural development, water supply and sanitation, environmental protection, urban development, and logistics. There are now 57 founding members of the bank, which, because of the great interest accruing to it, has also garnered support from many countries outside of Asia. While the biggest contributors are China, Russia, and India, Germany represents the biggest contributor among the non-Asian bank members.

The president of the bank will hold office for five years and may run for another term. The new president, Jin Liqun, has underlined that bank personnel will be chosen on the basis of merit, and the bank will be run in a strict manner aiming for profitable investment in infrastructure, which will also take full consideration of the economic effects of such investment. Lou Jiwei, China's Finance Minister, was elected as chairman of the bank's board of supervisors.

President Xi Jinping, who had initiated the project, gave the opening address at the launch of the bank. Speaking to the delegates, Xi underlined the overall significance of the founding of the bank as a new model of economic governance: "The founding and opening of the AIIB also means a great deal to the reform of the global economic governance system. It is consistent with the evolving trend of the global economic landscape and will help make the global economic governance system more just, equitable and effective."

The new bank, Xi continued, "will serve to channel more resources, particularly private investment, into infrastructure projects to promote regional connectivity and economic integration. It will bring along a better investment environment and more job opportunities and trigger greater medium- to long-term development potential on the part of developing members in Asia. This, in turn, will give impetus to economic growth in Asia and the wider world."

President Xi also announced in his speech that China would be contributing an additional $50 million to the capital of the bank for projects in less developed countries.

China's Premier Li Keqiang also addressed the delegates to the conference: "The aim of China initiating the AIIB is to widen financing channels, expand general needs and improve supply so as to bring along the common development in the region, and promote world economic recovery with its own achievements." The Premier called on the AIIB to integrate the China-proposed Belt and Road initiative with each country's development strategies, promote international cooperation on production capacity, and innovate more modes of realizing a diverse and inclusive cooperation.

The first projects of the AIIB will be announced before the end of the year, Jin Liqun told reporters. In addition, Mr. Jin said that the loans would be issued in dollars, although other currencies would be accepted for investment in the bank's capital, giving the lie to the propaganda that AIIB was an attempt by China to "internationalize" its currency, the RMB.

Membership in the bank is still open to other countries that might wish to join, including the United States and Japan, which have declined to become members. Initial attempts by the Obama Administration to pressure countries not to join the AIIB proved totally fruitless. South Korea, with which the United States has, like Japan, a defense treaty, is the fifth largest stakeholder in the AIIB. And even the Philippines, which has folded completely before U.S. attempts to bring U.S. troops back to the country, also felt obliged not to miss the boat and recently applied for membership in the bank.

Executive Order Makes Philippines U.S. Colony in Drive for China War

by Michael Billington

Jan. 13—The Philippine LaRouche Society chairman Butch Valdes yesterday denounced the decision by the Philippine Supreme to Court approve President Benigno (Noynoy) Aquino's treasonous deal with President Barack Obama, which turns Philippine military bases over to U.S. military occupation. The Court ruled the deal to be an "executive agreement" rather than a treaty, and therefore supposedly legal and constitutional, and therefore not requiring the approval of the nation's Senate.

The decision creates a Constitutional crisis, since the Philippines Senate voted in December that the agreement was clearly a treaty as defined by the Constitution, and must thus be approved by the Senate—which would likely vote to reject the criminal and suicidal agreement.

Lyndon LaRouche stated today that this agreement, if not stopped, constitutes a British recolonization of the Philippines through their agent Barack Obama. The entire process was run by Obama. It was signed during his visit to Manila in April 2014, and was intended to be approved by the Court during his visit in November 2015, but the huge opposition from the population and the Senate stalled that decision.

The agreement, called the Enhanced Defense Cooperation Agreement (EDCA), will allow the United States. to deploy its most advanced air, land, and sea forces, and weaponry into Philippine military bases, despite a clear Constitutional restraint on any foreign bases on Philippine soil without Senate concurrence.

The eight bases named thus far include Subic Bay and Clark Airfield (two primary U.S. bases used in the genocidal, failed U.S. war on Vietnam, Laos, and Cambodia), as well as two bases on Palawan Island, a Philippine island which juts out into the South China Sea. It makes a mockery of Obama's lie that China is militarizing the South China Sea by building up artificial islands with light houses and airstrips.

LaRouche added that the indication is clear that Obama intends to start World War III.

The statement by the Philippine LaRouche Society's Butch Valdes reads:

The Final Betrayal

The Filipino people have been betrayed yet again… not just by a demented president, nor by prostituted legislators, but by the very institution mandated to uphold, first and foremost, the Constitution of the Sovereign Philippine Republic.

Like fools and Judases, they hide behind faulty technical issues of the EDCA, twisting definitions, leaning on flimsy interpretations to manufacture their blatantly treasonous decision. Willfully blind to the true nature of the U.S. military installations inside Philippine Military Bases—which may very possibly be silos of nuclear-

U.S. Navy/Larry Foster

A view of the U.S. Naval Base at Subic Bay in the Philippines, as it was in 1981. It's been closed since 1992, but is now set to be reactivated.

armed medium/long-range rockets aimed at China—these justices of the Supreme Court commit treason of the highest degree against the Filipino people.

In my opinion, they have collectively sworn allegiance to a foreign occupying power which makes them moral cowards who do not deserve any iota of respect from the citizenry. The late Chief Justice, José Abad Santos, a true hero and patriot, turns in his grave to have these despicable characters in the same revered Halls of Justice.

To consciously place 100 million Filipino lives at risk in a nuclear conflict between two super powers earns for them the worst places in hell... and may they live long enough to experience the resulting pain and destruction which they have caused.

The referenced former Chief Justice José Abad Santos was the Chief Justice of the Supreme Court of the Philippines in 1941-42, and also acting President on behalf of President Manuel Quezon when Quezon went into exile in the United States after the Japanese invasion, on the advice of Gen. Douglas MacArthur. Chief Justice Santos stayed behind, but refused to capitulate to the Japanese occupiers' commands. The Japanese murdered him in 1942.

The comparison of the current U.S. military occupation of the Philippines to the Japanese occupation is absolutely correct, as the Japanese target was not the Philippines itself, but China and Asia generally—as is the case also with Obama.

The people of the Philippines will have a profound response to this accurate comparison. Will the U.S. population break through their degeneration to see what Obama is doing in their name, and remove him now, before it is too late?

The British Role

The British hand in this insanity traces back to the first days of the Twentieth Century. The U.S. had militarily liberated the country from its four centuries of colonization under Imperial Spain in the Spanish-American War in 1898. But rather than grant the Philippines its independence after an appropriate period of tutelage and support, the United States was convinced otherwise by the British, and especially by the British

EIRNS

Philippine LaRouche Society chairman Butch Valdes, addressing the first national conference of the Save the Nation movement in Manila in April 2013.

agent Theodore Roosevelt, who campaigned for the U.S. Vice Presidency in 1900 on a platform of making the Philippines the first colony of an imperialist America. Teddy Roosevelt won the election, and became President within six months, due to the British assassination of President William McKinley. The Philippines thus became an American colony, and America's decline commenced.

Only with the election of Franklin Roosevelt in 1932 did the independence of the Philippines become a reality. FDR's commitment in 1935 to grant the Philippines independence after a ten-year transition was upheld in 1946, despite the intervening hell of the War in the Pacific. Gen. Douglas MacArthur, who had lived in the Philippines as a youth when his father was Governor-General there, strongly supported independence, and went to the Philippines to build an army when the plan for independence was announced in 1935.

Now, the British imperial policy has again taken over the United States under British assets George Bush and Barack Obama. The recolonization of the Philippines will be regarded in history as a crucial moment in the process of degeneracy of the United States and the perversion of the American System.

The official Chinese government news agency Xinhua on Jan. 13 pointed to that degeneracy, writing that the deal will "make the Philippines a launching pad for U.S. military intervention in the Asia-Pacific," and will "only aggravate regional tensions and could push the situation to the brink of war."

mobeir@aol.com

IV. British Carnage in the Trans-Atlantic Region

Imperfect Economy: Italy's Struggle With the British Empire

by Claudio Celani

L'Economia Imperfetta
by Antonino Galloni
Movecento Editore, 2015
Paperback, €13.60

Jan. 17—My friend Antonino ("Nino") Galloni's latest book, *L'Economia Imperfetta*, is not his usual albeit brilliant economic essay, but almost an autobiography. This makes it particularly interesting, as it describes a life spent in the effort to influence the destiny of his own country by a young revolutionary initially, later a professor of economics, and a government official, and currently a civil servant.

Nino's story stretches through almost five decades of the social, political, and economic history of Italy and the world. It also intersects the political trajectory of his father Giovanni, a former government minister and national leader of the Christian Democratic Party (in Italian, Democrazia Cristiana, or DC). Giovanni Galloni is a representative of that generation of political leaders who successfully implemented "Hamiltonian" methods to transform Italy from a rural country into a leading industrial country in the postwar period. Enrico Mattei, Ezio Vanoni, and Aldo Moro are a few names of the leaders of that faction, which was sponsored by none other than the great Pope Paul VI, Giovanbattista Montini.

Montini and the leadership group he educated looked at the principles and policies of the Franklin Roosevelt Presidency in the United States as a successful implementation of the social doctrine of the Church, and laid them out in what is considered the founding document of the social and economic policy of the Christian Democratic Party, the 1943 *Codice di Camaldoli*. Later, Roosevelt's surviving circles retained their influence in Italy after the bestial Harry Truman had reversed Roosevelt's policies in Washington. Still later, John Kennedy was a supporter of Enrico Mattei and of Aldo Moro's project for a center-left government.[1] The historical connection of Franklin Roosevelt to Italian developments, played a role in Lyndon LaRouche's recruitment, many years later, to leadership of

---

1. See "Mattei and Kennedy: The Strategic Alliance Killed by the British," by Claudio Celani, *EIR*, June 5, 2009.

Antonino Galloni greets Lyndon LaRouche at a Schiller Institute conference in Germany in April, 2013.

the policy-making of the incoming first Ronald Reagan Administration.

The Italian system of the decades 1950-1980, in fact, although generally fitting in the category of a "capitalist" economy, was better characterized as a "mixed" system, with the state playing an active role as a kind of "entrepreneur" which did not pursue profit in itself, but as a result of the increase of the productive powers of society. Nino pays a tribute to this successful model, arguing that had it been continued, it would have "overcome capitalism."

Encounter with LaRouche

Unfortunately, the "Italian anomaly" ended abruptly with the kidnapping and assassination of Aldo Moro in 1978, in the context of a paradigm-shift in western culture and economy: the 1968 counterculture and the ensuing anti-science environmentalist movement, and the decoupling of the financial system from the physical economy.

Nino is one of a few Italian economists currently, such as Alberto Bagnai, Giulio Sapelli, Antonio Maria Rinaldi, and Paolo Savona, to name some of them, who are campaigning for an "exit strategy" from the Euro system. Like them, Nino has acquired growing popularity in the most recent years, especially after the shock of the EU-imposed austerity regime of Prime Minister Mario Monti (2011), which has cast Italy into a terrible depression. However, unlike his colleagues, Nino is not just an economist but an experienced expert on the government machine, having been in it at the top as director general of various ministries. Were Italy to reverse current policies and adopt an "exit strategy" from Hell, Nino is the man qualified for the job, either as Prime Minister or in charge of the economy.

Nino would not object to being called a "Keynesian," if by that one means being in favor of dirigistic investment policies. However, he refers to two figures who have influenced his views on the economy: his teacher Federico Caffè (1914-1987) and Lyndon LaRouche.

Federico Caffè was an anti-free market economist who educated an entire generation of economists, although not all are loyal to his teachings. A famous aphorism of Caffè, which he used to address those who invoked the power of "the market," was: "The Market has a name, a family name and a nickname." In his early days, Caffè was assistant to the chairman of the committee that drafted the current Italian Constitution,

Aldo Moro while a captive of the Red Brigades in 1978.

Meuccio Ruini, who published essays in praise of Friedrich List, the founder of the Hamilton-based National System of Political Economy.

Nino writes:

First and most important was for me the encounter with Federico Caffè, which occurred in 1980 after he had received from Prof. Edoardo Volterra my third booklet ("Crisis and Adaptation: for an alternative economic policy," a collection of articles I had written ... when I was in England and in the United States to study capitalism, and said that a certain Mrs. Thatcher and a certain Governor [Jerry] Brown in California were pushing ultra-conservative and insane ideas which, if implemented, would destroy the bases of our social fabric); after having read the text, Caffè told me that "rarely, in forty years of teaching," had he met "a person so versed in the matter," but "you could see from a distance" that I was "self-taught and, thus, they will make fun of you. I want to give you the school you need." Thus, this man who behaved like a father, dedicated two afternoons a week to me. I owe him almost everything.

Federico Caffè, Galloni's mentor.

Wall Street and Freedom we have the Ocean!"

All hell broke loose. My father was distraught. As we came home, he briefed my mother who said: "That was right. Bravo!"... [DC] Vice President Scaglione looked as though he wanted to beat me up, and would not calm down, even when I told him that, in my view, after so many mistakes, the U.S.A. would soon end up seeking Iran as strategic ally the region; 30 years later, I pushed the same idea at a meeting organized by Helga Zepp at the Schiller Institute, and Lyndon LaRouche complimented me for my "courage." ("Each time I see you I rejoice and I am astonished that they have not yet eliminated you.")

About his encounter with Lyndon LaRouche, Nino recounts how, in the early 1990s, a priest gave him a book to read and evaluate. The book was LaRouche's *The Science of Christian Economy*. The priest and an economist friend—

wanted to know from me whether I thought the work to be credible in its content; I told them that I was enthusiastic about it and wanted to become acquainted with the author, whence an intense relationship of friendship, mutual esteem, and collaboration was born. Thanks to LaRouche I have come to know wonderful people, sincere activists, first of all his wife Helga Zepp and Martin Luther King's collaborator Amelia Robinson, who have been often my guests and exchanged hospitality in Germany, Washington, and Los Angeles.

In another footnote, Galloni writes:

I remember some travels to the U.S.A., organized for my father in the late 1970s. Once, at Chase Manhattan Bank, 1 Wall Street, at the beginning of the Khomeini era, there was a meeting with David Rockefeller, who started saying "Our sister, Freedom" (the Statue of Liberty was visible from where he was speaking). I was close to the window and I interrupted him: "But really, from here I see that between

Called Back to Government

Nino distinguishes five phases of "capitalism" in postwar history:

(1) "The Expansive Model," from the 1946 Bretton Woods agreement to the 1979 G7 in Tokyo. This model was characterized by a high rate of technological progress and high salaries, as well as state welfare and services.

(2) "The Owners' Revenge," or we might say, "Rentiers' Revenge," from 1980 to 1992. This was a reversal of the previous trend, introduced with a policy of high rates of interest which advantaged the rentier class, resulting in a decreasing rate of technological progress and of a decreasing rate of growth of incomes, welfare, and services provided by government.

(3) "Financial Capitalism" in the classical sense, based on the maximization of financial values (stocks, bonds). This phase lasted nine years, from 1992 to 2001, when it collapsed.

(4) "Ultra-Financial Capitalism" (2001-2008) based on derivative schemes to keep the collapsed system alive.

(5) "Collateralized Ultra-Financial Capitalism," basically the same as before, but now backed by the unlimited guarantee of central banks, printing low-cost money in exchange for any kind of collateral offered by the banks.

The shift from the first to the second phase, as previously mentioned, occurred after the assassination of Aldo Moro, the former prime minister who, as chairman of the ruling Christian Democratic Party was negotiating for national unity on behalf of an independent economic and foreign policy.[2] Under Moro's chairmanship, Galloni's father Giovanni was Deputy Secretary General of the DC.

Two years after Moro's assassination, his policy collapsed and the neoliberals took power, starting a process that doubled national debt in a decade. This occurred through a combination of financial liberalization and a decreasing rate of investment in industry and infrastructure, in favor of "services." In particular, Treasury Minister Beniamino Andreatta and central banker Carlo Azeglio Ciampi implemented a *coup d'état*, by "decoupling" their two institutions.

With a simple letter sent by Andreatta to Ciampi, the Bank of Italy ceased to be the purchaser of last resort of government bonds, a measure that had thus far helped to keep interest low on the national debt. At the same time, capital controls were lifted, heedless of the fact that Italy's productivity, lower than its competitors, would result in capital outflows. This caused a skyrocketing of interest rates and yields on government bonds, which at one time reached over 20%.

Nino, who had quarrelled with Andreatta when the latter was at the Budget Ministry where Nino was an official, writes:

> That letter [by Andreatta to Ciampi], but especially its implementation by governor Ciampi, was more than a coup d'état, more than treason: Millions of youth could not aspire to a normal life because of it; industry has been abandoned, hundreds of thousands of firms have been forced to shut down; the State has become a simple operator desperately looking for financing, the Ministry of the Treasury has surrendered to the so-called market, i.e. the banks, its prerogative of determining interest rates.

In 1988, at a national meeting of the left-wing current of the Christian Democracy, Nino—who in the meantime had left the administration—intervened, saying that his forecast had been confirmed: National debt had doubled, and youth unemployment was at 50%. He received major news coverage, and one year later, he got a call from Prime Minister-designate Giulio Andreotti: "Dear professor, I think that you are right, we must change something in the economy. Do you want to help?"

Andreotti arranged a meeting between Nino and

Paolo Cirino Pomicino, his lieutenant in Parliament. "Giulio told me that we must change the economy of this country—what should we do?" Pomicino asked him in Neapolitan dialect. "Very simple," Nino answered, "Make sure that you are appointed Budget Minister in the next government, put me on top of the entire structure, and I will take care of the rest."

Thus, in August of that year, Nino was called back to the Budget Ministry as Director General and started immediately to work on a new draft of the budget, abandoning the monetarist approach which had been followed in the preceding years.

And Suddenly Fired

The course of Prime Minister Andreotti was clear: "The agreement with France, Germany, and Holland on fixed exchange rates should not lead to precipitating extreme and irreversible decisions which would damage our country; a certain priority of fighting against inflation should be maintained, while however establishing strategic lines which should allow a recovery of employment and of the Mezzogiorno," i.e., Southern Italy.

While working on the new policy document, Nino debated Mario Monti in Milan, and argued that an expansionist policy would not generate inflation because of the idle labor force and machinery.

Suddenly the weather changes. We are now in the crucial period of the Fall of the Wall, when London and Paris decided to force Germany to abandon monetary sovereignty in exchange for reunification. Andreotti's position shifted "from strongly eurosceptical positions to the opposite line." Nino believes that Andreotti, "because of his actions in economic and international policy (larger independence for Italy) was blackmailed by the Americans—who had listed our politicians as 'good' and 'bad' on the basis of short-sighted criteria—to force him to accept a radical downsizing of the defense of national interests."

The following scene plays out in the Minister's office: "I went to [Minister] Pomicino and, when he hinted we should not talk about it because we could be wiretapped, I took a piece of paper and wrote on it: 'Could it be that [Treasury Minister Carli] promised that if I go, you will become his successor?' Pomicino took the note, nodded and shredded it."

However, pressures came from much higher than Carli. Financial lobbies, corporations, kingmakers, and vested interests of all sorts placed their phone calls to Andreotti, but at one point, "the decisive phone call

---

2. See the author's "Strategy of Tension: The Case of Italy," *EIR*.

came, the one to which you could say neither 'no' nor 'let us wait,' nor 'let us reflect,' nor 'but,' nor 'if.' Someone had warned Helmut Kohl that there was somebody who 'opposed' the European project or the agreements …; I was forced to leave the task of advising economic ministers to other persons with a totally different approach."

What was the project which "somebody" in Rome was opposing? It was the Euro project with the Maastricht agreement, signed in 1992, but agreed to in November 1989 between France and Germany, which included:

(1) That Germany renounced the D-Mark in favour of a single currency, which freed the French political class from the shame of being able to, and being forced to devalue; (2) in exchange, France accepted Germany's reunification; and (3) Italy should be disempowered and deindustrialized so that, although for different reasons, both France and Germany could see in the future of the single currency (and of its attached rules) the lesser evil for them.

A large responsibility for signing the treaties, however, lies on those Italian representatives such as Treasury Minister Guido Carli, who believed in the "external constraint" which would "discipline" Italian governments into running balanced budgets. Such a thought by foreign interests could be understandable, but not on the part of such Italians, whom Nino calls "collaborationists."

The Maastricht/Euro project was doomed to fail, and did fail with "Financial Capitalism" in 2001. It was kept alive through financial derivatives ("Ultra-Financial Capitalism"), but this scheme also blew up in 2007-2008, and it has been kept alive so far only through the central bank lifeline, "Collateralized Ultra-Financial Capitalism," which is driving the U.S. government to consider the idea of a thermonuclear war as a feasible "solution."

How can Italy and humanity can be saved from this perspective? Even if the BRICS countries succeed in "leading the process of saving humanity, the latter cannot avoid (1) a reintroduction of the strict separation

In the 1990s, Galloni was given LaRouche's 1991 book, The Science of Christian Economy, *by a priest, who asked him to evaluate it. Thus began "an intense relationship of friendship, mutual esteem, and collaboration" with LaRouche.*

between credit and finance"—by which the Glass-Steagall Act is meant; "(2) a sterilization plan for existing toxic assets (for instance, withdrawal and freezing of the latter, with emission of credit aimed at new investments); and (3) development strategies in the various sectors—environment, medicine, education, infrastructure, culture, maintenance of housing and health—supported by a re-establishment of the monetary sovereignty of states."

The last point is a central issue for Italy, faced with certain death inside the Euro system.

Nino has three possible scenarios for an exit strategy from the Euro:

Plan A is "the consensual exit from the Euro"; Plan B is "a non-consensual exit, supported by international agreements able to contain speculative attacks"; and Plan C, if both A and B are not politically feasible, is the creation of "parallel" currencies, followed by "a progressive loss of power" of the Euro.

The Imperfect Economy

Nino's reference to "environment" as a priority item for investments should not confuse the reader. Throughout the book, he makes it clear that environmental policies based on Malthusianism, anti-science, and climate-change ideologies are to be fully rejected. Only through technological innovation and an increase of the "energy intensity" of the system is it possible to protect the environment.[3]

Nino goes so far as to expose the "original sin" of progressive forces which at one point in history decided to ally with environmentalists and bankers to defeat industrialism as a perceived enemy. This was decisive in creating the political conditions that defeated the alliance which had implemented the model of "expansive capitalism." The Left did not understand that had it supported that alliance instead, it would have achieved what it considers to be its objective: overcoming capitalism.

If we accept the common definition of capitalism as

---

3. See Galloni's comment on the recent papal encyclical, *EIR*, July 3, 2015.

The Enrico Fermi nuclear power plant in Trino, Italy in 2010. All of Italy's nuclear power plants have been shut down as a consequence of the Maastricht agreement, signed in 1992, which called for Italy to be deindustrialized.

a system based on individual profit, we must recognize that there are still forces today, in the Italian economy especially, but also in other countries, which strongly contradict such a proposition.

Under the combined effect of the financial crisis and the Euro austerity policies, Nino writes:

> Large industries in Italy have virtually disappeared: 75% of the famous state-owned corporations (which were admired throughout the world because they were different and more efficient than classical government-run enterprises) have been somehow lost, that is to say sold at wholesale prices; small enterprises have been reduced by 25% (as compared to the turnover at constant values in the period preceding the steep decline); the infrastructure system is in a state of abandonment (with interesting exceptions for railways); and public services are steadily compromised by various necessities (tax cuts, imaginary reforms, persecution of state employees, and sponsorship of the lucrative "competition" by private interests).
>
> Nevertheless and despite that, the de-industrialization of the country seems to be neither complete nor satisfactory for European competitors: enterprises of small and very small dimensions keep producing and innovating, ensuring continuity for exports and export-substitution. Unlike small and very small enterprises in France and Germany, in fact, Italian firms do not lack efficiency, and do not exclusively operate in the domestic market.
>
> And yet, except for some rare exceptions, they have neither had help from the banks nor from the Administration, nor could they rely on an infrastructure system adequate to the times and to the international rank of their country, and they have suffered from situations of [failure of] public order and legality....
>
> Considering that only 10% of their balance sheets are in the black, and under the conditions listed above, the most important issue to raise is the following: If 90% of small and very small enterprises in Italy, though efficient from a market standpoint, are not producing profits ..., why do they continue to produce; why do they not close shop?
>
> Any economics textbook would suggest selling the business and living on interest or dividends; instead, those small and very small entrepreneurs decide to control real resources (even by adopting behaviors which, at the financial level, would seem to be irrational), maintain a role and a dignity in society, and ensure some form of employment to the members of their families, and not only them.
>
> We are talking about four million families, over ten million workers .... If we add to these heroes the millions of farmers, including those not counted among the labor force, housewives, and volunteers in aid of persons and environment, we begin to get an idea of an economy which does not pursue profit, but is of major significance and effect in the country, and has a balanced budget but allocates various kinds of resources to productive activity.

Is that "capitalism," or something else? Certainly it is a purpose higher than profit, a purpose that defines man as different from beasts. This is what, despite everything, is holding society together and is the potential waiting to be mobilized to produce a renaissance.

Regime Change in Germany?

by Rainer Apel

Jan. 18—An unprecedented New Year's Eve incident at Cologne's main railway station which badly shocked the German public, was in actuality nothing other than a British bid for regime-change against Chancellor Angela Merkel,—part of an attempt to destroy Germany along with its potential resistance to British plans for war.

Following a riotous scene with fireworks shot into crowds of people in front of the Cologne main station in the late hours of Dec. 31, massive, orchestrated assaults were carried out upon women, involving theft and sexual offenses committed by criminal gangs of "North African-looking men." This entire affair has shaken the German population from Jan. 5 on, as if, for instance, a terrorist bomb attack had been carried out against the world-renowned Cologne Cathedral. The shock has been enhanced by sensationalist media reports and hurried law-and-order statements coming from leading politicians, and reports of a number of intense police raids on certain corners of bigger cities which have traditionally been frequented by men from northern Africa.

But more important: the Cologne shock has triggered a stream of calls for a complete change of German policies on refugees generally, in particular refugees from Islamic countries; calls for changes in the direction of a militarization of the police, even the use of the armed forces inside the country; changes also toward more rigid controls along the Mediterranean borders of Europe; and finally, steps to keep refugees entirely out of Europe.

Targetting a Stumbling Block

These calls for completely reversing Chancellor Merkel's wise decision of last year to welcome refugees to Germany and provide for their needs, amount to calls to topple her government. They are in fact calls for Merkel's replacement by the likes of her bestial, London-linked Finance Minister Wolfgang Schäuble of the "black zero,"—that is, the balanced budget at all costs.

Don't ignore the fact that it is the British Empire, with its Saudi satellite, which has the means to create provocations both from Salafists, and from anti-immigrant mobs like the German "Pegida," which are linked to the British Intelligence-infiltrated English Defense League and English soccer hooligans.

Insiders know that once Germany says "no," most geopolitical designs in Europe won't work; so far Germany has only said "yes, but...." Still, that underlines Germany's potential opposition to London, rooted in a remaining spark of economic potential which is unfortunately unique in the trans-Atlantic area today.

And one should not overlook the fact that a crucial tool of the London-centered imperial monetarist faction, the extreme budget-cutters' current in German

Chancellor Angela Merkel's diplomacy with Russian President Putin makes her a prime target for the British Empire. Here Merkel and Putin meet in Paris in October of 2015.

kremlin.ru

politics around Finance Minister Schäuble, has come under massive domestic pressure to step back, because Germany needs more homes, schools, repair work, and new investments in the public infrastructure—to support and integrate the one million refugees that have come to Germany in 2015. Furthermore, the notorious "black zero" faction around Schäuble has come under pressure to release funds for a postwar economic reconstruction program in Syria (where 50% of the refugees have come from) and Iraq.

No Benefit

After the Cologne incidents, policy-makers in Germany have been engaged in heated law-and-order discussions, one trying to outdo the other, and an increasing militarization of the debate has taken place in the mainstream media, in TV talk shows, and in public political events. Schäuble has reiterated earlier initiatives of his to demand the deployment of the armed forces inside Germany, many others have called for the army to shield Germany's borders with the rest of Europe against refugees, and there are proposals to create giant internment camps in the southern EU member countries for refugees, in case several hundred thousand of them should try to come to Europe this year, as in 2015.

And from these internment camps, hundreds of thousands of refugees are to be deported back to where they came from. This would never work, but it is being proposed nevertheless, particularly by German leaders, many of whom opposed taking in so many refugees during 2015 in the first place.

If Germany capitulates to the British Queen, the one behind the New Year's Eve attacks in Cologne, it would not benefit, but would instead be sacrificed on the altar of monetarism along with all other nations, since her goal is all-out thermonuclear war between NATO and Russia.

That cannot be allowed to happen. The LaRouche movement in Germany has begun an intense political campaign to force the public debate back onto reasonable tracks, prominently addressing the fact that the only weapon that makes any sense is the bank separation weapon, the reinstatement of the Glass-Steagall Act to shut down Wall Street and allied British Empire assets.

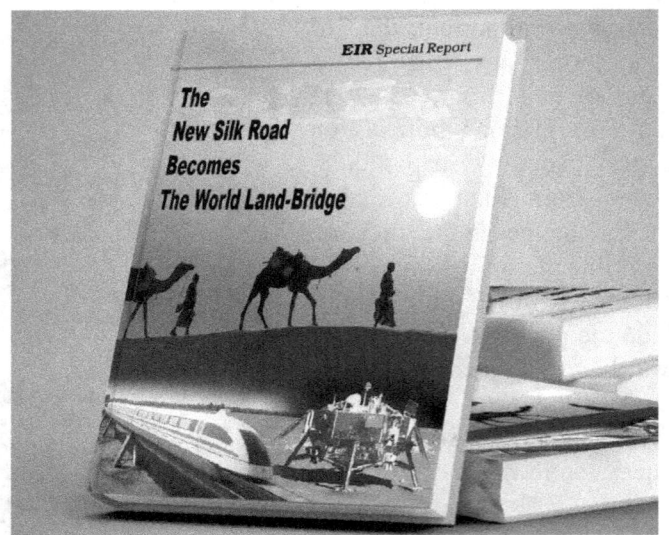

Turkey: NATO's First Rogue State

by Dean Andromidas

Jan. 19—Turkey has become the North Atlantic Treaty Organization's first "rogue state." This term, so popular with the State Department and the neo-conservatives, is used against states with alleged "authoritarian" regimes that supposedly support terrorism and seek weapons of mass destruction. Turkey's President, Recep Tayyip Erdogan, is increasingly being recognized as an "authoritarian" whose government is supporting the Islamic State of Iraq and the Levant (ISIL) in Syria. And now it is reported by specialists in Washington and London that Erdogan is calling for the development of an independent ballistic missile capability with a range of 3,000 km, far enough to hit almost any target in the European Union and the western half of Russia.

Saudi-U.S Relations Information Service

Turkey's President Recep Tayyip Erdogan hosts Saudi King Salman at his palace on March 2 2015.

This confirms Erdogan's own statement of intent on ATV television on Nov. 18, 2015.

But unlike Saddam Hussein's Iraq, or North Korea, Turkey is a member of NATO—it could drag the alliance into World War III. Many were reminded of this ugly possibility when, on Nov. 24, Turkey became the first NATO country since the formation of the alliance to shoot down a Russian warplane without provocation.

In Whose Behalf?

But make no mistake, this "clear and present danger" is not the folly of the former mayor of Istanbul, who has delusions of becoming the Sultan of a resurrected Ottoman Empire, but is rather the work of the Anglo-Saudi empire that has thrown the entire Middle East into war and catastrophe that, if not stopped, promises to lead directly to a thermonuclear confrontation between Russia and the West.

Just as the old Ottoman Empire was manipulated by

the British Empire against Russia and its other rivals, today's Turkey has become that same tool against Russia. Since Russia made its strategic move into Syria to crush ISIL and end the civil war, Turkey has taken the lead in the attempts to stop it, under orders from its Anglo-Saudi masters. The shooting down of the Russian warplane was only the most dramatic and dangerous ploy.

In what is nothing less than a war crime on behalf of the Anglo-Saudi empire, Turkey is using the millions of Syrian and other refugees—which its support of the war against the Syrian government has generated—against Europe. It is an open secret that the Turkish authorities have allowed the people-smugglers to operate freely along its coasts, generating waves of hundreds of thousands of refugees into the European Union. most of them via impoverished Greece.

Greek President Prokopios Pavlopoulos, in an interview with the Germany daily *Süddeutsche Zeitung* published Jan. 18, on the occasion of his official visit to

Germany, accused Turkey of facilitating the smuggling of migrants.

"I have serious concerns that Turkish human traffickers get support from authorities," Pavlopoulos told the German daily. "In particular, port authorities are pretending to be unaware of this."

That this humanitarian catastrophe is being used as blackmail against particularly Germany, the one country seeking cooperation with Russia on these issues, was exposed by Turkish Deputy Prime Minister Mehmet Simsek himself, in an interview with Germany's *Die Welt* on Jan. 16: "If Germany and others want to stop the influx of refugees, they must stop the bombing against the Syrian opposition." The "Syrian opposition" to which Simsek refers are Turkmen, most of whom are Turkish nationals—such as the Turkmen terrorist who murdered the Russian pilot of the Su-24 shot down last November in his parachute—or are mercenary Turkmen from central Asia.

In an expression of caution from the side of the U.S. military, the daily *Defense News* noted Turkey's likeness to a rogue state in its report on Jan. 16 that Erdogan is seeking long-range ballistic missiles. It also quoted an unnamed, Ankara-based NATO ambassador, who expressed his concern that "Such ambitions can fuel sectarian tensions in the region. A missile rivalry between a NATO member Turkey and Iran does not sound pleasant."

Turkey as Pakistan

With the outbreak of the so-called Arab Spring in 2011, Turkey's foreign policy of "zero problems" with neighboring countries became that of the chief standardbearer for the Muslim Brotherhood takeover of the entire Middle East. When the Arab Spring hit Syria, Turkey under Erdogan went from being a "strategic partner" with Syrian President Bashar al-Assad to becoming the logistical base for the massive, Saudi-financed military operation to overthrow the Syrian Government.

Again, the mastermind was not the would-be sultan, but is seen in a very clear deal Erdogan signed with the Anglo-Saudi monstrosity known as the Sunni alliance, which led to billions of dollars pouring into Turkey, not only to pay for the war against Syria, but also to keep Erdogan in power. It is no secret that Erdogan's Justice and Development Party won the last election thanks to billions of dollars that poured into the country during the election campaign, money that originated in Saudi Arabia and Qatar.

Erdogan renewed his membership in the Sunni alliance last December, when Turkey announced it was joining the 34-nation, Saudi-backed so-called Islamic military alliance against terror. Erdogan's official visit to Saudi Arabia followed on Dec. 29, when the two countries agreed to set up a "strategic cooperation council" to strengthen military and economic cooperation between the two countries.

Four days after this visit, on Jan. 2, Saudi Arabia conducted its infamous execution of 47 prisoners it called called terrorists, including the country's leading Shi'a cleric, Nimr al-Nimr, an atrocity that Iran saw as a major provocation, and which reinforced the widespread belief that the Saudi-led "Islamic military alliance against terror" is nothing more than the sectarian Sunni alliance that has been backing the overthrow of the Syrian government and taking aim at Iran and its influence in the region.

As with any pact with the devil, the policy has come with a bloody price. In a February 2015 interview with the Turkish daily, *Today's Zaman*, retired British MI6 officer Alastair Crooke warned that Turkey could become like the Pakistan of the 1980s under pro-Muslim Brotherhood President Muhammad Zia ul-Haq, who suffered serious blowback from the same terrorist organizations he had sponsored, also with Saudi money, to fight the Soviet forces then occupying Afghanistan. These were the same groups that later morphed into the Taliban and al-Qaeda, backed by the same Saudi networks responsible for the 9/11 attacks on the New York World Trade Center and the Pentagon.

Crooke, who is director and founder of Conflicts Forum and former adviser on Middle East issues to former EU Foreign Policy Chief Javier Solana, told the Turkish daily that the Turkish government's strategy for playing a leading role in the region may be costly, because Turkey might become hostage to ISIL.

"I was there at that time," Crooke said. "Zia ul-Haq was a strong, Muslim Brotherhood-oriented leader, and he rejected any notion of blowback. For 25 years, I have seen political leaders who believe that they can control and use the Salafists for their own ends, but who subsequently find it is they who have been used by the Salafists."

Zia ul-Haq paid the supreme penalty for his policy. He died in 1988 in the crash of the C130 transport aircraft in which he was travelling. The official inquiry found that the most probable cause of the crash was sabotage.

Blowback on Turkey

Almost one year after that interview, Crooke told *EIR* for this article that he believes the situation in Turkey in this respect is even worse than it was in Pakistan in the 1980s. Erdogan's courting of ISIL and the Salafists has seen these forces penetrating the entire "fabric of the state," as it is well known that MIT, the Turkish National Intelligence Service that takes its orders from Erdogan, has been supporting Islamic terrorist operatives in Syria. Now these groups have "leverage," and any attempt to curtail their operations is very dangerous. Crooke pointed to the recent Istanbul suicide bombing targeting the city's most important tourist site—in which 10 German tourists were killed—as a case in point.

Although this was the first attack on tourists, the Istanbul bombing is only the latest of several high-level terrorist attacks in Turkey, including one last summer in Ankara, Turkey's capital, that killed more than 100 people.

Crooke went on to assess the very seriously deteriorating situation in Turkey. He warned that it is just a matter of time before Erdogan's war against the Kurdistan Workers Party (PKK)—which has led to civil war conditions in the country's southeast and which he used to win the elections—spreads to the western districts of Turkey. The Istanbul bombing was a foretaste of such violence. On top of this violence is the collapse of the economy. Erdogan's economic policy has been based on real estate speculation and hot money. The former has collapsed, and the latter is being pulled out of the country, as Turkey is seen descending further into chaos.

Another point of internal instability is the "internal polarization" Erdogan has created. This includes the repression of all criticism of the government, such as the arrest and dismissal of academics who signed a petition calling for an end to the heavy security operation in the southeast. The opposition to Erdogan has spread to elements in the ruling Justice and Development Party itself, which Erdogan does not hesitate to repress brutally.

Proxy War with Russia

Turkey's shooting down of the Russian Su-24 warplane last Nov. 24 has highlighted the fact that Turkey has launched a proxy war with Russia since the latter made its strategic intervention against Turkey and its Anglo-Saudi sponsored ISIL and other terrorist organizations. The attack on the Su-24 has led to NATO taking over the defense of Turkey's airspace bordering Syria with the deployment of NATO's AWACS surveillance planes and maritime patrol aircraft and ships provided by Germany and Denmark, while Spain will deploy its Patriot surface-to-air missiles along Turkey's border to replace those recently removed by Germany and the United States.

Under the cover of NATO's security umbrella, Turkey believes it can continue to channel support to ISIL and other terror groups operating against the Syrian government and Russian forces, including their smuggling of oil from ISIL-controlled oil fields in Syria. None of this has deterred Russia and Syria from carrying out their operations against ISIL in Syria, which are said to be achieving considerable success.

Turkey has facilitated the movement of thousands of anti-Russian fighters—who are wanted in Russia for terrorism—from the Russian Caucasus to fight in Syria as well as their return to conduct terrorist operations in Russia itself. It is also feared that Turkey is stirring up mischief among the ethnic Turkic population in Crimea and Central Asia, including the Turkic Uyghurs in China.

In the volatile Caucasus, Armenia—a member with Russia of the Commonwealth of Independent States—has asked for, and received assurances from Russia for support against any possible Turkish attack. While Armenia has no border with Russia, it does border Turkey and Turkey's ally Azerbaijan, with which it has a long-running dispute over the Nagorno-Karabakh enclave in Azerbaijan. In consequence of this request, Armenia and Russia have integrated their air defense systems and Russia recently announced it will deploy MIG-29 fighter jets and a Mil Mi-8 transport helicopter to a Russian base near Yerevan by the end of this year.

Russia has also made diplomatic representations to Azerbaijan to prevent any rise in tension between Azerbaijan and Armenia. It is believed that Azerbaijan, despite pressure from Turkey, has no stomach to get involved in such insane schemes.

Russia, while refusing to be provoked, has nonetheless responded with increasing economic pressure on Turkey. While imposing sanctions on certain Turkish exports to Russia, tightening visa requirements, and suspending new construction projects, it has virtually ended Russian vacationing in Turkey. Russia has also suspended the construction of Turkey's first nuclear power station as well as all nuclear-related research and training programs.

The Russian government also invited the co-chair-

Kurd Press

Turkish Army troops mobilize to pursue Kurdish fighters in the Qandil Mountains. The Kurdish fighters are among the most effective against the Islamic State.

man of Turkey's People's Democratic Party (HDP, oriented to the Kurdish issue), Selahattin Demirtas, to Moscow last month, where he met with Russian Foreign Minister Sergei Lavrov. According to Sputniknews.com, Demirtas said during this meeting that Turkey should not have shot down the Russian Su-24 last month and that Turkey should work to improve relations with Russia.

"We criticized the government's actions when it downed the Russian plane," Demirtas said. "Problems between states will always arise, but it's necessary to leave the door open for a political and diplomatic settlement," Demirtas added, whose party has 59 seats in the 550-seat Turkish parliament.

The visit did not please Erdogan, who immediately called Demirtas a traitor.

Civil War in Turkey

Erdogan's reckless policy is leading to the "Syrianization" of Turkey itself. For weeks, in the cities of Turkey's ethnic Kurdish southeast, war has been raging between Turkish security forces and the PKK, and several cities have been kept under curfew. This warfare has led to scenes of destruction similar to Aleppo and Homs in Syria. Every day the body count increases, with deaths of members of the security forces, PKK fighters, and civilians. While more than 100 civilians have been killed in the last months, the Turkish army admits to the death of well over 200 members of the security forces and more than 500 PKK fighters.

The protracted security operations have caused an uproar among the Kurdish community and the opposition more broadly. More than 1,200 academics have signed a petition demanding an end to the security operations and a return to negotiations with the PKK, which the government broke off last year. Erdogan's response has been to conduct brutal repression, arresting several of the signatories on charges of supporting terrorism, while demanding that university rectors dismiss signatories.

The conduct of the Erdogan government has drawn a strong response from the main opposition, the Republican People's Party (CHP). Its leader, Kemal Kiliçdaroglu, slammed the Turkish government in a speech given shortly after the Istanbul suicide bombing.

"No buts about it, from now on, 78 million citizens in Turkey need to know this truth: This government cannot govern Turkey. It is not able to govern. The Twenty-first Century's Turkey cannot be ruled with third-degree staff. We have so far remained silent and we have been patient. Now we have run out of patience; you will go if you are not able to rule, and those who are able to rule will take over," Kiliçdaroglu said in an address before his party's parliamentary group.

He said his party had warned the government years ago not to "drag the country into the Middle East quagmire."

An Army Insider Sums It Up

Lt. Col. (ret.) Mithat Işik, former head of the elite Turkish army unit Bordo Bereliler (Crimson Berets), slammed the government's anti-Syria policy for dragging Turkey into a security disaster, in an interview with *Today's Zaman* on Jan. 12.

"Turkey has tried to design Syria in line with its foreign policy priorities without considering Syria's own social dynamics. These wrong policies have resulted in the emergence of state-like structures that pose a threat to Turkey's domestic security. Broken relations with Russia, Iran, Iraq, and Syria have turned Turkey into a main target for the terrorist groups in question. The government should abandon its policy of undermining its neighbors' interests and should cooperate with them, in order to prevent future attacks," Işik said.